Where Are the Women?

Gender Equity, Budgets and Canadian Public Policy

Janine Brodie and Isabella Bakker

CCPA
CANADIAN CENTRE
for POLICY ALTERNATIVES
CENTRE CANADIEN
de POLITIQUES ALTERNATIVES

Library and Archives Canada Cataloguing in Publication

Brodie, M. Janine, 1952-
 Where are the women? : gender equity, budgets and Canadian public policy /
Janine Brodie and Isabella Bakker.

Includes bibliographical references.
ISBN 978-1-897569-05-4

1. Canada--Social policy. 2. Fiscal policy--Canada. 3. Women--Government
policy--Canada. 4. Women--Canada--Social conditions. 5. Social security
--Government policy--Canada. 6. Social security--Government policy--
Canada--Provinces. 7. Government spending policy--Canada. 8. Canada--
Politics and government--1993-2006. 9. Incomedistribution--Sex differences
--Canada. 10. Gender-based analysis--Canada.
I. Bakker, Isabella C. II. Canadian Centre for Policy Alternatives III. Title.

HQ1236.5.C2B758 2008   361.6'10820971   C2008-905199-8

Printed and bound in Canada.

Canadian Centre for Policy Alternatives
Suite 410, 75 Albert Street, Ottawa, ON K1P 5E7
TEL 613 563-1341 FAX 613 233-1453
ccpa@policyalternatives.ca
http://www.policyalternatives.ca

Contents

About the Authors

Dr. Isabella Bakker is a professor of political science and political economy at York University, Toronto, Canada. She was a 2004–05 international Fulbright New Century Scholar. She has worked extensively with the United Nations on two UNDP Human Development Reports, with UNIFEM on the first Progress of the World's Women and with the Division on the Advancement of Women on gender mainstreaming in the budget and planning process of the United Nations.

Dr. Janine Brodie is a professor of political science at the University of Alberta. She was elected as a Fellow of the Royal Society of Canada in 2002, and awarded the Canada Research Chair in Political Economy and Social Governance in 2004. Before joining the University of Alberta in 1996, she was appointed as the first director of the York Centre for Feminist Research and held the John Robarts Chair in Canadian Studies at York University. She also was the University of Western Ontario Visiting Chair in Public Policy.

Preface

MAJOR PARTS OF this policy research paper were proposed and developed under a call for proposals issued by the Policy Research Fund (PRF) of Status of Women Canada (SWC) in September 2004. The final report, entitled *Canada's Social Policy Regime and Women: An Assessment of the Last Decade*, was peer-reviewed, edited, translated into French, and scheduled for publication in early 2007. It was not published, however, because the newly-elected Harper government both cut the operating budget of SWC and terminated its Independent Policy Research Fund (PRF). Initially established in 1996, this fund supported gender-based policy research on public policy issues in need of gender-based analysis with the goal of developing equitable policy. During its decade-long lifespan, the PRF funded and published over 75 studies, which had proved to be critical resources for policy-makers, policy advocates, and equality litigants. The abrupt and arbitrary cancellation of the PRF has effectively put an end to the capacity of SWC to generate independent policy research and to assemble external expertise to advocate for women's equality and gender equity inside and outside of the federal government.

In the fall of 2006, the Honourable Beverley Oda, then Minister of Canadian Heritage and the Status of Women, defended the cancellation of the PRF and budget cuts to SWC before the House of Commons Standing Committee responsible for the status of women. She argued that the new Conservative government "does fundamentally believe that all women are equal." Contrary to Minister Oda's assertion, this report underlines that the goal of gender equality has not been met and, importantly, that the relentless attack on federal social programs over the past decade have undermined the goal of gender equity, as well as the well-being of Canadian women, especially the most vulnerable.

Research generated by Statistics Canada in 2006 also indicates that, on a variety of fronts, gender equality remained an elusive goal of public policy. *Women in Canada: A Gender-based Statistical Report* (Statistics Canada 2006) noted that the increased participation of women in the paid workforce, and especially of women with young children, was one of the most significant social trends of the past 30 years. In 2004, 58% of women aged 15 and over were employed, while the participation rate among women with children under three (65%) and children aged three to five (70%) had effectively doubled since 1976. Still, the report found that, compared to their male counterparts, women were far more likely to lose time at work because of personal or family responsibilities, work part-time, and earn less. In 2003, Canadian women working full-time (full-year) earned 71% of what men working full-time (full-year) earned. Similarly, 38% of families headed by lone-parent mothers lived below the poverty line, compared to 13% of male lone-parent families, and 7% of two-parent families. Statistics Canada also reported that, in 2004, females were six times more likely than males to be victims of sexual assault and far more likely to experience criminal harassment, stalking, and spousal abuse (*CCPA Monitor 2006, 29*).

Our initial report can be found on the SWC website at http://www2. swc-cfc.gc.ca/qfsearch/SearchServlet?encoding=ISO-8859–1&collection= Internet&sortfieldo=relevance&lang=en&queryo=brodie+and+bakker.

The initial report, as well as this revised report, reflect the views of the authors. However, we wish to thank SWC for funding this research and Jo Anne De Lepper and Zeynep Karman, formerly of SWC, for their support of and contributions to this project. Parts of the postscript can be found in Brodie (2008b).

Executive Summary

THIS REPORT ARGUES that contemporary social policy reforms, while often attributed to the ongoing pressures of economic globalization, the ascendance of neo-liberal thinking in political and policy circles, and broader shifts in the economy, labour markets and social structures, also have been accompanied by the progressive disappearance of the gendered subject, both in discourse and practice. Most recently, Canada's minority Conservative government, elected in January 2006, declared that the goal of gender equity had been achieved and then purged any reference to gender equality from the mandate of Status of Women Canada. However, as this report underlines, the degendering of social policy and the erasure of the goal of gender equity from the policy process has been a more long-standing project, reaching back to the mid-1990s. In fact, government accountability to gender equality goals (e.g., The Federal Plan of Action, Beijing+10, and the Convention on the Elimination of All Forms of Discrimination against Women) has been marked by a significant disconnect for more than a decade. This disconnect, or policy *in*coherence, is signaled by both the pursuit of "gender-neutral" policies, such as tax expenditures (which we demonstrate to have very gendered outcomes) and, the declining capacity to undertake gender -based analysis (GBA) in key areas of fiscal and social policy. The erasure of gender, we argue, has significant implications for other key policy commitments, such as the eradication of child poverty. Another consequence is the repudiation of the amassed feminist research of the social sciences, which has repeatedly documented the implicit gendered norms that underpin supposedly gender-neutral models and assumptions, particularly in fiscal policy.

This erasure of gender, we argue, is partly attributable to the priority given to market accountability and sound macroeconomics. Questions of social cohesion, poverty reduction, social and gender justice have taken on a secondary import; any attention to these issues is seen as conditional to the realization of a sound fiscal picture. We suggest that all macroeconomic policies are social policies with distributional consequences along regional, gender, race and class lines. The general political and economic context within which social policy decisions are framed limits the ability of equality-seeking groups to make claims on public resources.

This report focuses on five dimensions of this degendering process. Part 2 of the report examines the progressive residualization of social policy since the early 1990s. Major federal social policy initiatives are discussed and evaluated in terms of their implications for different groups of women. Another related policy shift in federal social policy in the last decade has been the almost exclusive focus on children. As we illustrate, the National Child Benefit and other social tax expenditure measures are linked to broader objectives of social welfare reform that promote labour force attachment among welfare recipients and only indirectly invest in children.

Part 3 of the report focuses on factors we identify as contributing to the fragmentation and erosion of Canada's social assistance regime and relates this to an analysis of their gender-differentiated impacts and outcomes. We review provincial and territorial changes over the last decade and focus on a nuanced understanding of poverty differentials and links to so-called gender-neutral public policies. The gendered underpinnings of poverty are examined, as well as the constraints of contemporary social policy regimes that help entrench a poverty trap for Canada's most vulnerable. Tax-delivered social policies, we demonstrate, do not benefit low-income women since they generally do not have enough taxable income or tax liability to claim deductions, exemptions, or credits. Family-directed tax expenditures, such as the Canadian Child Tax Benefit, also assume that the primary breadwinner shares financial gains equally within the family, an assumption that ignores many micro-studies on intra-household financial inequalities.

Part 4 of this report documents the degendering of policy capacity, both within and outside of government, and relates this to the disappearance of women in the reform of the post-war social policy regime. We refer to this process as the 3Ds of degendering policy capacity: delegitimization, dismantling and disappearance. This threefold process, we argue, stands in stark contrast to the international and national commitments of Canadian governments to undertake gender-based analysis and promote gender equality across the broad spectrum of public policy.

An increasingly important component of social policy capacity is the entire process of budget planning; this is discussed in Part 5 of the report. The last decade has been characterized by fiscal policy decisions that marked a period of dramatic cuts between 1994–95 and 1996–97, followed by a surplus era (1998–) where previous cuts were not significantly redressed. Indeed, in the surplus era the federal government has focused on two policy instruments to influence social policy: tax credits/refunds and federal-provincial/territorial agreements that involved earmarked unconditional increases to the CHST.

From a gender analytical perspective, we explore several key issues linking social policy to the budget process, including the federal government's unilateralism with respect to social policy decisions through the budget process. The fiscalization of social policy has largely taken place behind the veil of budget secrecy. Social policy has not been open to public consultation, nor have indicators, social audits, or shared best practices been developed in a systematic way that would concretize the principles of the Social Union Framework Agreement.

A series of recommendations related to the governance of social policy are provided in Part 6 of this report. These recommendations are designed to:

- enhance the capacity of gender units within government;

- re-insert national standards and mechanisms for consultation and accountability in the design and delivery of social policy reform;

- enhance the capacity of Canadian governments to conduct effective gender-based analysis; and

- reform budget planning and consultation processes to create gender-sensitive oversight mechanisms within the Department of Finance, which take into account gender-equality commitments in the distribution of resources.

Part 7 of this report is a postscript that describes significant changes to the gender equity envelope since the election of the Harper minority Conservative government in January 2006.

One

Introduction

IN RECENT DECADES, Canadians have witnessed pronounced economic and political transformations that, for many, have contributed to a growing sense of insecurity and uncertainty about the future. This section of the report examines one dimension of the changing parameters of the Canadian experience, notably, the transformative and ongoing changes to Canada's social policy regime and their implications for Canadian women. Pressures to reform Canada's social policy regime, which took shape in the post-war years and matured in the 1960s and 1970s, have been linked to the ascendance of neo-liberal thinking, both in partisan politics and within policy-making circles, and to broader shifts in the Canadian economy, labour markets, and social structures. It is now commonly argued that these latter factors have rendered the post-war model outdated, unsustainable, and ineffective. Economic globalization is attributed with reducing the capacities of government to shield its citizens from the realities of ever more competitive international markets, while Canadian society itself is increasingly marked by different types of work, new family forms, increased cultural diversity, and pronounced changes in both intra- and inter-generational life courses. These and other factors associated with what has been termed "the new economy" and "post-industrial society" have fuelled ever louder calls, in Canada and elsewhere, for new social programs and a new "social architecture" that can respond to the new social risks and insecurities of the 21st century (Jenson 2004).

A large and diverse range of policies and programs is subsumed under the broad umbrella of social policy, including health care, education, training, housing, income support, unemployment insurance, and care. Moreover, in Canada's federal system, primary responsibility for many of these policy areas rests with the provinces, others with the federal government, while still others are shared, if not in law then in practice. During the past century, however, the federal government largely took responsibility for social security programs, such as Unemployment Insurance, Old Age Security, the Guaranteed Income Supplement for the elderly, the Canada Pension Plan, the spousal allowance, and child and veteran's benefits. A second critical role for the federal government has been providing the provinces with cash transfers and tax points to assist in the funding of health care, post-secondary education, social assistance, and related social services (Rice 2002: 112). Third, the federal government has often taken a leadership role in conceptualizing the goals of social policy, as well as the substance of citizenship equality.

This report examines changes in the federal role in the social policy field, focusing on the impact of these changes on Canadian women and on gender-based capacity within Canada's federal and provincial governments. Part 2 of this report recounts key social policy changes since the federal Social Security Review (SSR) was launched in 1994. It represented an initial attempt by the federal government to re-think the goals, programs, and delivery of Canada's post-war social architecture. Many Canadian social programs, however, had already been significantly eroded in the previous decade through what social policy analysts have called the "politics of stealth," that is, cutting social benefits through fiscal policies and behind the veil of budgetary secrecy (Gray 1990). Beginning in the mid-1980s, the federal government regularly raised the spectre of the 3Ds — **dollars**, **deficits** and **debts** — as reasons for eroding the foundations of the postwar welfare state. The federal social envelope was progressively deprived of funds, the Unemployment Insurance program was repeatedly restructured to reduce benefits and tighten eligibility, and universal social programs for families and the elderly were subject to clawbacks and de-indexation (Torjman 1995: 1). During these years, the federal government, claiming the need for budgetary affordability and predictability, also began to retreat from its fiscal obligations to the provinces (at least the wealthiest provinces) to share equally in the costs of social assistance programs for Canada's most vulnerable citizens.

In many ways, then, the process of social policy reform was already set in motion before Prime Minister Jean Chrétien announced, in 1993, that social policy reform would be a priority of his newly-elected majority government. The launch of the Social Security Review (SSR) in early 1994 was applauded by some policy advocates as an opportunity to realize significant and necessary social policy reforms. Within a year, however, it was clear that the project of social policy reform would be eclipsed by federal budgetary manoeuvres that effectively dismantled the fiscal foundations of Canada's post-war social security and welfare systems. As Part 3 of this report explains, the cumulative impact of changes in the funding, delivery and design of social programs, at both the federal and provincial levels, has left in their wake an increasingly fiscalized, fragmented and eroded social architecture. As a result, Canada's poorest — disproportionately women and children, Aboriginal peoples, and visible minorities — are poorer and more financially insecure than they were before the reforms were enacted (NCW 2005).

Part 4 of this report documents the degendering of policy capacity, both within and outside of government, and relates this to the disappearance of women in the reform of the postwar social policy regime. We refer to this process as the 3Ds of degendering policy capacity: delegitimization, dismantling and disappearance (Brodie 2007). This three-fold process, we argue, stands in stark contrast to the international and national commitments of Canadian governments to undertake gender-based analysis and promote gender equality across the broad spectrum of public policy.

Part 5 elaborates on the gendered impacts of the progressive shift in power and influence in the policy-making process away from social equality concerns to the budgetary process.

It reviews how the assumptions of orthodox economics has systematically excluded a plurality of diverse expertise and interests in the budgetary process and created an incoherent policy environment that silences the articulation of gender policy concerns. This section also explores alternative models that would facilitate "bringing gender back in" to this critical centre of policy formation and implementation.

Part 6 provides a set of policy recommendations designed to enhance the capacity of gender units within government, to re-insert national standards and mechanisms for consultation and accountability in the design and delivery of social policy reforms, to enhance the capacity of Canadian governments to conduct effective gender-based analysis and reform the budget planning and consultation processes.

Part 7 summarizes significant shifts in discourse and policy in the governance of gender since the election of the minority Conservative government in January 2006.

Two

Canadian Social Policy Reform (1994–2006)

THIS SECTION FOCUSES on federal initiatives in the areas of social security and social assistance since the early 1990s, although selected changes in provincial social assistance programs are also reviewed. Table 1 provides a summary of the major social policy initiatives undertaken by the federal government during this period. Early in this period, federal social policy reform was characteristically fragmented, tentative, and driven by budgetary considerations, both in rhetoric and in fact. However, after the federal government began to record budget surpluses, beginning in 1998, the federal government launched a series of initiatives, both with and without the provinces and territories, to "repair the social union" (Prince 2003: 127). The following highlights the most significant innovations in social policy since the 1994 Social Security Review, among them the Canada Health and Social Transfer (1995), the National Child Benefit (NCB), and related child-centred programs, such as the Multilateral Framework on Early Learning and Childcare (2003), the Social Union Framework Agreement (1999), the Canada Social Transfer

(2004) and the Universal Child Benefit (2006). We begin with the Social Security Review.

The Social Security Review

Although commentators point to the progressive residualization of social policy in Canadian politics since the early 1990s (Prince 1999: 157), the period, in fact, began with the promise of a far-reaching and inclusive consultative process which, in the words of then Finance Minister Paul Martin, would culminate in "the most comprehensive reform of government in decades."[1] At the beginning of its mandate, in January 1994, the newly-elected Chrétien government announced its intention to "rebuild the social security, labour market, and learning framework of the country."[2] The Standing Committee on Human Resource Development was directed, by a unanimous vote in the House of Commons "to consult broadly, to analyze, and to make recommendations regarding the modernization and restructuring of Canada's social security system, with particular reference to the needs of families with children, youth, and working age adults."[3] From the outset, the SSR, described as the "largest public consultation in the history of Canadian social policy," elected to ignore, in its terms of reference, the gendered and often biased underpinnings of the existing social security regime, as well as ongoing gender disparities in income, employment, and well-being.

After months of consultation, involving the presentation of approximately 200 briefs, the House of Commons Standing Committee released its discussion paper, *Improving Social Security in Canada* (ISSC), in October 1994 (Jennissen 1996: 240). This discussion paper set out three principle objectives for comprehensive social policy reform.

- **Jobs:** Helping Canadians to get and keep work.

- **Support for the most vulnerable:** Providing income support for those in need, while fostering independence, self-confidence and initiative, and starting to tackle child poverty.

TABLE 1 *Major Federal Social Policy Initiatives (1994–2005)*

1994	Social Security Review (SSR)
1995	Canada Health and Social Transfer (CHST)
1996	Unemployment Insurance renamed Employment Insurance (EI)
1997	1997 Multilateral Framework on Employability Assistance for People with Disability (EAPD)
1998	1998 National Child Benefit (NCB): Canada Child Tax Benefit (CCTB) and National Child Benefit Supplement (NCBS) Canada Millennium Scholarship Foundation (Canada nd) Caregiver Tax Credit (CTC)
1999	Social Union Framework Agreement (SUFA)
2000	National Children's Agenda (NCA) Early Childhood Development Initiative (ECDI) Maternity and parental leave extended to 50 weeks
2003	Department of Human Resources Development Canada is divided into departments of Social Development Canada (SDC) and Human Resources and Skills Development Canada (HRSDC) Child Disability Benefit (CDB) Multilateral Framework on Early Learning and Child Care (ELCC)
2004	Compassionate Care Benefit (CCB) CHST divided into Canada Health Transfer (CHT) and Canada Social Transfer (CST)
2006	2006 New Department of Human Resources and Social Development Canada (HRSDC) created with merger of SDC and HRSDC Universal Child Care Benefit (UCCB)

- **Affordability:** Making sure the social security system is within the government's means and more efficiently managed, with a real commitment to end waste and abuse (HRDC 1994: 10).

Grounded in a human capital rather than a citizenship equality model of social governance, ISSC represented a significant departure from postwar thinking about social policy goals and programs. In a sense, the ISSC sketched out a framework for Canada's "third way" by advancing an "activist" social policy agenda that promised to release poor Canadians from welfare dependency through employment programs, skills development, and income assistance for the most vulnerable, especially children (HRDC 1994: 10). According to the ISSC's analysis, poverty should be understood as being rooted in a skills deficit among individual adult Canadians. The ISSC explained that having few skills or the wrong skills locks potential workers out of the labour force, deprives them of "the satisfaction and dignity of work," and forces dependence on social assistance (HRDC 1994: 25). Social welfare reform thus should involve "building bridges to work — to independence, not dependence" (Canada 1994).

The assertion that social assistance recipients, disproportionately women, were dependent on welfare was already a familiar refrain among conservative thinkers in the United States. Tracing this discourse in the American context, Fraser and Gordon (1994) argued that this dependency metaphor carries a barrage of negative images that stigmatize the poor and assign them personal responsibility for their poverty. Both poverty and social assistance are viewed as evidence of an individual's shortcomings, and thus both blameworthy and avoidable.

Three policy options follow from this perspective:

- Access to social assistance should be tightened, and welfare clients should be facilitated or forced into the paid labour force.

- Because women, especially single mothers, are more likely to be recipients of welfare, reform strategies should focus on getting them back into the labour force.

- Only those unable to work, notably children and the severely disabled, are considered blameless for their poverty and, thus, are legitimate claimants to social assistance (Brodie 1995: 58–61).

The ISSC's active welfare model was roundly criticized by many social policy advocates, both for its narrow conceptual framework and for its dismissal of gendered care work as central to its analysis. Most women (and men), as it was underlined, do not enter the labour force as unattached individuals, but rather as members of a family unit, with few supports for their caring activities (Kitchen 2005: 20). Little attention, however, was afforded to the value of women's reproductive and caring work, and the constraints that these responsibilities impose on women attempting to enter or already in the paid work force. Others took issue with the ISSC's underlying messages that paid work was the only legitimate activity for the non-elderly, and that social programs were disincentives to work and a burden on taxpayers and employers (Torjman 1995: 2–3).

The discussion paper raised similar concerns among women's advocates, both inside and outside the government. During the consultation phase, the Standing Committee had been urged repeatedly to take gender into account in its report. In December 1994, Human Resources Development Canada (HRDC) hosted a national women's consultation in which about 80 women's groups participated. This meeting emphasized the need for the federal government to take into account Canada's commitments to women's human rights in the formulation of a new social security regime. The National Action Committee of the Status of Women (NAC) and the Federation des Femmes de Québec (FFQ) joined forces to host a two-day conference in Regina, which produced 12 principles to guide the social policy review (Teghtsoonian and Grace 2001: 250–251). Similarly, the Canadian Advisory Council on the Status of Women (CACSW) commissioned several research notes on social policy reform and pressed the government to adopt a gender-sensitive framework. The CACSW reminded the Standing Committee that "Canada's domestic and international commitments to women's equality require governments and their advisors to adopt a gender-sensitive framework for all aspects of their work."[4]

Many provincial women's organizations also presented briefs to the House of Commons Standing Committee. For example, in a joint submission, the advisory councils of New Brunswick, Nova Scotia, Prince Edward Island, and Newfoundland and Labrador argued that the ISSC's proposed changes have tremendous implications for women, their work, and their relationships with their families and the state. However, this fact is not acknowledged anywhere, nor is there any understanding that women will be affected differently than men by the proposed changes to Canada's social programs. Most disturbing is the discussion paper's assumption that all women in Canada share the same experience and common needs (Joint Submission 1994: 3).

Despite these numerous and diverse interventions, the SSR's final report, *Security, Opportunity and Fairness: Canadians Renewing Their Social Programs,* released in February 1995, made few concessions to the concerns of social policy advocates or representatives of the Canadian women's movement. Among the report's 52 recommendations, only the last eight addressed concerns about women's equality. There were concessions, for example, to incorporate gender-sensitive analysis, and to accommodate the specific needs of women and other disadvantaged groups "in the design and delivery of employment services" (Canada 1995: 80).

In retrospect, as discussed in Part 4, the report signaled the beginning of the erasure of women as a distinct constituency in the development of social policy in Canada. While repeatedly urged to "take women into account," the final report was, in fact, a model of *gender insensitivity* that ignored gender as a socially relevant variable in policy-making (Jennissen 1996: 239). Throughout the report, women were degendered through such universal terms as "Canadians, individuals, family members, clients, and working adults," and then regendered as welfare dependents who, by the very fact of receiving social assistance, possibly posed a threat to their children's future (Teghtsoonian and Grace 2001: 251; Brodie 1995: 59–60). As the ISSC explained, "the price of staying on welfare is high... children who grow up on society's sidelines risk the continuation of a cycle of low achievement and joblessness" (HRDC 1994: 70). These threads of degendering and individualization, which ran through the final report, were only possible because the report did not recognize the "link between gender and structural inequality" or that women variously situated by, for example, marital status, ability, age and race, often confront different kinds of obstacles in the labour market, and in Canadian society more broadly (Jennissen 1996: 241). The term "potential employable" dismissed both persistent gender inequalities *between* women and men and growing disparities *among* Canadian women themselves.

The Canada Health and Social Transfer

The debates generated by *Security, Opportunity and Fairness: Canadians Renewing Their Social Programs* were rendered moot a few weeks later with the announcement of the Canada Health and Social Transfer (CHST) in the 1995 federal budget. To the surprise and alarm of many social policy advocates and provincial and territorial governments, then Finance Minister Paul Martin announced that the federal government intended to withdraw from 50-50 cost-sharing of provincial social assistance programs by reducing federal funds marked for social assistance and combining them with a pre-existing block grant designated for health care and post-secondary education. The CHST replaced two of the foundational fiscal pillars of Canada's postwar social architecture: Established Programs Financing (EPF) and the Canada Assistance Plan (CAP). As such, it represented a historical watershed in the evolution of Canadian social policy (Bakker and Brodie 1995).

Ottawa had initially stepped back from the principle of cost-sharing with the provinces with respect to post-secondary education and health care in 1977, with the establishment of the EPF. Unlike cost-sharing, which matches federal dollars with provincial dollars spent in designated areas, the EPF was a block grant transferred directly to provincial consolidated revenue funds, calculated on a per capita basis, and consisting partly of tax points and partly of a federal cash transfer. The federal government attached no conditions to the post-secondary component of the EPF, while payment of the health component was conditional on compliance with the principles set down in the *Canada Health Act*. These are universality, comprehensiveness, portability, accessibility, and public administration. Provinces failing to comply with these principles can be subject to federally imposed penalties. Not surprisingly, perhaps, post-secondary institutions soon felt the brunt of the new block fund as provincial governments directed their spending to the more politically popular health care sector and to other provincial priorities, including tax cuts.

The CHST represented a significant change in the existing social policy architecture because it eliminated the Canada Assistance Plan. Introduced in 1966, CAP formally combined four federal-provincial cost-sharing programs: the 1952 *Old Age Assistance Act*, the 1952 *Blind Persons Allowance Act*, the 1954 *Disabled Persons Allowance Act*, and the 1956 *Unemployment Assistance Act*. Importantly, CAP also extended cost-sharing to provincial mothers' allowance programs and to welfare services, including child welfare services. The elimination of CAP also ended federal cost-sharing in other key areas important to women, such as social housing, home care, and shelters. Under CAP, the federal government committed itself to a 50–50 cost-sharing formula with all the provinces except Quebec, which exercised its option to opt out of federal programs in return for tax points.

At the time of its introduction, CAP was applauded for consolidating the existing patchwork of provincial and federal social assistance programs and for providing a relatively uniform national social assistance infrastructure with minimum national standards in welfare provision. The Canada Assistance Plan required that social assistance be provided to persons without minimum residency requirements or obligations to work, and that there would be an appeals procedure. More critically, CAP insured the right of all Canadians, regardless of their personal circumstances, to the collective provision of a social minimum — to food, fuel, clothing and shelter — on the basis of need alone. CAP was also a critical social program for Canadian women, especially for single mothers who were more likely than their male counterparts to depend on provincial social assistance regimes to meet their daily needs and those of their children.

The late 1980s and early 1990s saw pronounced increases in the number of Canadians seeking social assistance, which, in turn, put additional strain on the budgets of both the federal and provincial governments. In 1993, for example, there were one million more Canadians on some form of social assistance than there had been a decade earlier. In Ontario, fully 11% of the population was on some form of social assistance (Rice 1995: 189). In 1990, the federal government attempted to partially contain its open-ended financial commitment to social assistance by imposing a ceiling on its social assistance transfers to the "have" provinces of Ontario, Alberta ,and British Columbia, with the so-called "cap on CAP." In the same year, the federal government also ended its financial contributions to the Unemployment Insurance(UI) program with respect to benefits tied to regional job markets, tightened the benefit structure and redirected funds to such "active measures" as vocational training (Campeau 2005: 127–130). As Campeau argued, through a series of UI reforms implemented in the early 1990s, "the government hijacked the [UI] system away from its priority mission of compensating the jobless and its primary role as a social insurance plan." Unemployment Insurance premiums were increasingly diverted "from the specific purpose for which they were collected" (Campeau 2005: 127).

At first glance, then, the introduction of the CHST might be viewed simply as an instrument of fiscal federalism, "a child of federal deficit reduction and cousin of provincial demands for greater autonomy in social policy" (Prince 2003: 141). But it also was much more than a modality of fiscal federalism. The CHST represented the federal government's unilateral withdrawal from 30 years of practice in the funding of Canada's social assistance programs, as well as an announcement that the federal government intended to reduce its contributions to the provinces in social welfare, health, and post-secondary education. The CHST also represented the end of the federal government's previous commitments to Canada's most vulnerable, including the right to obtain assistance on the basis of need alone, and the right to appeal.

The CHST is often remembered for its dramatic cuts in cash transfers to the provinces, which dropped from $17.4 billion in 1994–95 to $12.4 billion in 1997–98 (Yalnizyan 2005a: 33). Moreover, unlike the EPF and CAP, the CHST did not contain an escalator formula for the cash portion of the transfer; growth in the cash component of the block fund would depend on "federal largesse" (McIntosh 2004). Indeed, it was not until 2000–01 that the cash component of the CHST returned to its 1995 level, largely as a result of a "one-time" and targeted deal with the provinces to prop up health care spending. Pressure from both the voting public and the provinces prompted the federal government to pump additional funds into health care again in 2003 and 2004 (Yalnizyan 2005a: 61).

The CHST has been indicted for, among other things, increasing both the depth and incidence of poverty, diverting social assistance funds to health care and children, as well as fragmenting and eroding Canada's social safety net (Evans 2002: 82; Prince 1999: 178). As described in detail in Part 3, these and other factors do characterize Canada's social policy terrain a decade after the introduction of the CHST, but these outcomes were not necessarily dictated by the new block fund. Instead, the CHST is best viewed as an *enabling fiscal instrument* rather than a determinant of the kinds of social programs that have evolved in recent years. As discussed later in this report, the substance of welfare reform has been influenced by other factors, not the least the ascendancy of neo-liberal governing assumptions and the dominance of heterodox economics in the budgetary process. Moreover, the federal government's hand in the erosion of the post-war social safety net certainly was not limited to either the creation of the CHST block fund or to the reduction of cash transfers to the provinces. The 1995 budget, for example, also announced severe cuts to federal departmental spending that were even larger than the proposed cuts to provincial social transfers. Although many federal programs were "deeply retrenched," Human Resources Development Canada (HRDC) was hit the hardest. Its budget was reduced by about 35% ($2.8 billion over three years), accounting for two-thirds of the cuts in federal social programs (Yalnizyan 2005a: 29–30).

With the return of budgetary surpluses, new federal program funding has not, for the most part, flowed back into the social field. As Yalnizyan (2005a: 75) reported, federal department spending increased, cumulatively, by $42 billion in the surplus era (1998–2004), but only two programs, Defence and the Canadian Opportunities Strategy (cos), comprise the bulk of the total increase in federal departmental spending. Described in the 1998 Budget Speech as "a co-ordinated set of measures" "designed to create opportunity by expanding access to lifelong learning," cos funds such innovations as the Millennium Scholarship Foundation and the Canada Foundation for Innovation. However, precisely because these programs are housed within a foundation, it is difficult to determine who benefits from these programs (Yalnizyan 2005a: 82–89). The first 2006 budget of the minority Conservative government also enhanced military spending, targeting $5.3 billion in new money in the next five years (Den Tandt 2006: A14). By 2007, defence spending reached levels not seen since the early 1950s at the height of the Korean conflict and Cold War.

Un/Employment Insurance

In 1996, the federal government continued to alter Canada's social architecture with critical changes to the Unemployment Insurance program, which was renamed Employment Insurance. The UI program had been steadily eroded throughout the 1990s when the rules governing eligibility were tightened, coverage periods shortened, and benefits reduced. As a result, the percentage of unemployed Canadians receiving UI benefits dropped from 74% in 1990 to 51% in 1994 (Den Tandt 2006: 36). The 1996 reforms introduced important structural changes, making hours instead of weeks worked the basis for calculating eligibility. On the face it, the shift to hours potentially benefited women workers. As of 2003, 17% of Canadians worked part-time, and 69% of these were women. Indeed, the women's part-time employment rate increased from 24% in 1976 to 28% in 2003 (compared to 11% of men in 2003) (swc 2005).

TABLE 2 *Gender Differences in EI Receipt among the Unemployed*

	1994	1996	2001
Women	49%	39%	33%
Men	53%	45%	44%

Source Yalnizyan (2005a: 36).

On closer inspection, the 1996 reforms made it more difficult for both women and men paying into the program to qualify for benefits. Under the 1994 rules, a worker needed the equivalent of 300 hours of paid work to qualify for UI benefits. The 1996 rules, however, required anywhere from 400 to 900 hours of work, depending on local employment rates, to qualify for benefits. Combined with changes in contribution periods, under EI, many part-time workers "would have to pay more into a fund that they were increasingly unlikely to be able to access for help" (Yalnizyan 2005a: 35). Charges that the 1996 reforms would put EI benefits further out of reach for unemployed workers, especially women workers, were soon confirmed, as shown in Table 2. Since 1996, the proportion of unemployed workers receiving EI benefits dropped by 9% among men and 16% among women. In 2001, only a third of unemployed women were receiving EI benefits.

Employment Insurance surpluses ballooned in the late 1990s and the early years of the new millennium, and the federal government came under increasing criticism, from such divergent sources as trade unions and the Auditor General of Canada, for directing these surpluses from insecure and unemployed workers to other governmental priorities, especially debt repayment. Indeed, in 2003, labour unions mounted a court challenge against the federal government, arguing that, in 2000 alone, $7.2 billion of the employer–employee financed fund went to unemployed workers while $8 billion went to general revenue. They charged that, by 2003, EI premium overpayments accounted for $45 billion of the $47 billion the government had spent paying down the debt (Beauchesne 2003: A5).

In 2000, the EI program was revised to extend maternity and parental leave for the care of newborn and newly adopted children to a maximum of 50 weeks (plus a two-week qualifying period). About 90% of claimants for maternity and parental leave are mothers and, in 2003, about 65% of mothers with children less than one year of age benefited from this much applauded federal initiative. Nonetheless, because the leave program pays only 55% of previous earned income, it tends to advantage moderate- to high-income as well as dual-income earner families. Statistics Canada data show that women with lower incomes tend to return to work much sooner (within four months) than those with higher incomes (nine to twelve months). Moreover, self-employed and contract women workers did not have access to this option. Somewhat paradoxically, other federal government initiatives have aimed at increasing the number of self-employed women in Canada, but, as it now stands, they are not covered under the EI maternity and parental leave program (Yalnizyan 2005a: 72; Townson 2005: 4–5).

Innovations in social policy, which attempt to accommodate growing family-work balance issues, are necessary as greater numbers of women with young children enter the paid labour force. Some 63% of mothers with children under three years of age are in the paid labour force compared to 53% in 1990 (SWC 2005). Yet, it is worth noting that the current maternity and parental leave program is both uneven in its coverage and privately financed through employee and employer contributions to the EI program. Setting aside the debate about whether this is an appropriate source of funding for what is, in effect, infant care and family policy, it is clear that additional sources of public funding are needed to ensure equitable maternal leave periods and incomes for all new parents, as well as to build public infrastructures for infant and child care. In a bilateral agreement with the federal government, Quebec established a provincial parental insurance program which addresses some of the weaknesses of the existing federal program. Begun in January 2006, the new program includes self-employed workers and provides up to 75% of previous earnings for new parents. Importantly, as Townson (2005: 5) explained, higher benefits will be available for low-income parents while eligibility will not depend on hours worked.

Another federal policy aimed at reducing family/work stress, the Compassionate Care Benefit (CCB), shares some of the same weaknesses as the parental leave program. Announced in 2004, the CCB changed the Labour Standards Code to allow employees who have worked for at least three months to take a six-week unpaid leave to care for a family member who is seriously ill and has a high risk of dying within 26 weeks. Some workers, caring for their family members, are eligible for six weeks of paid leave through the EI program, within a 26-week period, but only if they have 600 insured hours and can demonstrate that their weekly incomes have declined as a result of their caring activities. In 2006, the plan was altered to allow for a broader range of family members, notably sisters and brothers, to access this program and to share in caring responsibilities. Nonetheless, applicants must be EI-eligible to participate in the program. As already discussed, these restrictions may be prohibitive for many women who work part-time or who cannot afford to forfeit income to care for a dying family member. Equally important, the CCB does not recognize the ongoing family/work strains experienced by workers with frail parents or with severely disabled family members who need constant care but are not in immediate risk of dying. Although the federal government does provide some financial relief through the tax system for the costs of caring for disabled family members, Canadian governments have yet to seriously consider a long-term care insurance similar to that introduced by Germany in 1995 or by France in 2004 (Kitchen 2005: 20).

National Child Benefit and Children's Agenda

During the past decade, children have been almost the exclusive focus of federal social policy initiatives. This singular focus on children, especially children "at risk," finds its roots in the UN's World Summit for Children (1990) and the Mulroney government's 1989 pledge to end child poverty in Canada by 2000. This was the same government that only a year before had ended the universal family allowance, once a cornerstone of Canadian family policy. Child poverty rates actually increased from the 1989 level of 14% to 22% in 1996. This rate fell to about 15% at the turn of the millennium, dropping to about 13% in 2004 (Rice 2002: 102; Kitchen 2005; Statistics Canada 2006). Canada's child poverty rates, however, remain high when compared to those in other OECD countries with similar levels of prosperity.

The federal government tentatively attempted to redress this persistent problem with the introduction of the Child Tax Credit in 1993 and, again, with much more bravado, in the 1997 federal budget, with the introduction of the Canadian Child Tax Benefit and the National Child Benefit Supplement. Falling under the broader umbrella of the National Child Benefits system, the CCTB and the NCBS were soon followed by a series of other child-focused initiatives, many undertaken in concert with the provinces and the territories, including the Early Childhood Development Agreement (ECDA) (2000), the Child Disability Benefit (CDB) (2003), the Multilateral Framework on Early Learning and Child Care (ELCC) (2003), and the Universal Child Care Benefit (UCCB) (2006).

As a tax expenditure, the CCTB provides a refundable tax credit for families with children below a specified taxable income, while the NCBS provides additional support for low-income families with children. In July 2003, for example, a CCTB of $1,169 was clawed back at $33,487 and the NCBS of $1,463 was clawed back at $21,529 (Paterson et al. 2004: 132). The federal government announced significant increases to the CCTB in its 2003 budget, with benefits for the first child increasing to $3,243 by 2007. Families caring for a child with a disability also are eligible for the CDB, but only if their income falls below a particular threshold. In 2003, the maximum CDB of $1,600 had an income threshold of $33,487. In the 2006 federal budget, the CDB was increased to $2,300. Overall, total expenditures on federal child benefits have been targeted for a 60% increase in the decade between 1997 and 2007 (Battle et al. 2003: 2).

The implementation of a child tax benefit had previously been recommended by the Social Security Review, social policy advocates such as the Caledon Institute, and the provincial ministers of social services (Dobrowolsky and Jenson 2004: 171). Designed in collaboration with the provinces, territories and First Nations, the NCBS was intended to advance three policy objectives:

- prevent and reduce child poverty;

- ensure families are better off as a result of parents working; and

- reduce overlap and duplication of government programs and services (Rice and Prince 2004: 123).

The NCBS represents the costliest social tax expenditure in the period under review, amounting to $15 billion between 1998 and 2004, but this constitutes only about 10% of total tax expenditures implemented in these years (Yalnizyan 2005a: 80). Similar to tax cuts, the NCBS effectively bypasses the provinces and provincial programs by providing additional income to individuals and families. However, the NCBS implicitly involves an indirect federal–provincial transfer. Under the deal, the provinces are allowed to adjust their payments to those on social assistance by the amount provided by NCBS and use these savings to support other programs and services for low-income families. Thus, the NCBS does not provide additional income for all Canadian families on social assistance. Moreover, there are few mechanisms to ensure that the provinces do, in fact, redirect these savings into programs for Canada's most vulnerable. There is also no way to track whether these savings encourage the provinces to provide benefits to poor families that they would not have otherwise provided.

Under these circumstances, a strong case could be made that the CCTB and the NCBS have more to do with providing the working poor with marginally better incomes and resources than those on social assistance, rather than with ensuring all Canadian children have some degree of horizontal equity and opportunity. Such "making work pay" or "welfare in work" initiatives implicitly recognize that many jobs available in contemporary labour markets do not generate sufficient income to provide a sustainable family wage. The NCBS, in other words, is intricately tied to the broader objectives of contemporary social welfare reform to promote "labour force attachment" among welfare recipients and only indirectly to investing in children (Dobrowolsky and Jenson 2004: 171). The lack of any accountability mechanisms to determine how the provinces redirect any social assistance savings also suggests that the NCBS serves to replace some of the social assistance funds taken away from the provinces with the termination of CAP and federal–provincial cost sharing in this field.

The Early Childhood Education Development Agreement unveiled in September 2000 represents an additional federal–provincial/territorial initiative which, unlike the CCTB, targets funds and programs more directly and transparently toward children. The centrepiece of the new National Children's Agenda — worth over $2.2 billion over five years or $100 for every Canadian child — was designed to build the capacities of governments, non-governmental organizations, First Nations and local communities to provide supports for families and children in four broad areas:

- healthy pregnancies, births, and infants;

- parenting and family supports;

- early childhood development, learning and care; and

- community supports (Phillips 1999: 113).

Importantly, the terms of this intergovernmental agreement do not tie federal funding to provincial performance with respect to the above goals. As Yalnizyan reported, in the first year of the agreement, the provinces added little additional money to this initiative (a mere $18.6 million) and used federal funds in many different ways, some only marginally related to the above policy goals. For example, together, the provinces and territories spent only 8% of the total fund for 2000–01 ($300 million) on expanding regulated child care spaces. Manitoba and the Atlantic provinces concentrated their funding on child care facilities while Canada's richest provinces, British Columbia, Alberta and Ontario, directed none of their funds to this policy priority. Instead, Ontario used the new monies to fund school milk programs (Yalnizyan 2005a: Table 14, 68).

The provision of accessible, affordable, and quality child care is widely recognized as a critical public infrastructure to address childhood development, child poverty, and the feminization of poverty. This social infrastructure provides children with equitable early learning environments and enables parents with young children to re-enter the labour force, and to retain earnings. Canada, however, has been singled out as a laggard among OECD countries with respect to the provision of child care. According to the OECD's most recent statistics, only 20% of all Canadian children under 6 years of age (and 12% of children under the age of 12) had access to regulated child care. This contrasts with rates as high as 78% in Denmark, 60% in the United Kingdom, and 40% in Portugal (Hunsley 2006: 11).

While affordable and accessible child care is a critical issue for most Canadian families with young children, it is especially so for sole parents (mostly women), many of whom live in poverty. The OECD notes that sole parents in Canada face particularly difficult choices when attempting to find and maintain employment and care for their children. Without any other option for viable child care, many single parents are forced to choose between the proverbial rock and a hard place: either take part-time work that, while providing flexible hours, also has low pay and few benefits, or accept inadequate provincial social assistance. Both options are a formula for the sustained feminization of poverty and for child poverty.

While the provinces have implemented various forms of child care subsidies, especially for poor families, Quebec stands out as a policy leader in the Canadian context. The province is building a universal child care system whose goal is to provide regulated child care for all parents who wish to use it, for a minimal fee. Although the supply of spaces has not kept up with demand, the province's allocation to early learning and child care far surpasses the commitments of other provinces in this area —$1.2 billion in 2005 alone (Laghi 2005: A3). Moreover, in January 2006, the province implemented the Régime Québécois d'Assurance Parentale

(RQAP). This program, unique in Canada, provides benefits for every eligible worker — salaried and self-employed — for maternity leave, parental leave, paternity leave or adoption leave. The plan allows new parents to select between two options: a longer leave period with lower benefits and a shorter leave period with higher benefits. Importantly, the RQAP eliminates the two-week qualifying period, which continues to be required by the EI scheme, it significantly increases the maximum insurable income, and it admits workers with as little as $2,000 insurable income.

Partially in response to both domestic and international insistence, the federal government and the provinces began to move tentatively toward a national child care program in 2003 with the signing of the Multinational Framework on Early Learning and Child Care. After sustained federal-provincial negotiation, this was followed in 2004 by the Early Childhood Development and Education Initiative (ECDE). Although separate five-year agreements were concluded with the provinces before the January 2006 federal election, the election of a minority Conservative government has brought significant changes to the development of child care policy in Canada. The Harper Conservative minority honoured the former government's child care commitments to the provinces for only one year, and in its place has implemented a new Universal Child Care Benefit (UCCB).

A fiscal social policy instrument, the UCCB provides a taxable $1,200 a year (or $100 a month) for all children under 6 years of age. This universal benefit, which is expected to cost about $2 billion annually, is a significant tax expenditure. But it has been criticized for favouring two-parent families that can afford a stay-at-home parent to attend to child care needs. Because the benefit is taxable off the income of the lowest-paid spouse, families with one spouse, either unattached or minimally attached to the paid labour force, will realize larger financial gains from the program than two working parents, or single parents in the work force. In other words, this program effectively subsidizes a particular family form: the male breadwinner model. The UCCB also has been criticized for failing to provide adequate public support for building an early learning and child care infrastructure in Canada. Although the plan provides $250 million annually to create new spaces, especially in private sector workplaces, child care advocates argue that this allocation is inadequate to meet current need and demand. Monica Lysack of the Child Care Advocacy Association of Canada assesses the UCCB as follows: "A family allowance is great, but to call it child care is an insult."[5] Initial evidence indicates that the private sector has been slow to take up incentives to provide child care for employees.

Also termed the "choice in child care benefit," this proposal is yet another example of the fiscalization of social policy (Galloway 2006). It is represented as a universal social benefit — a reinvestment in the Canadian social fabric — that respects the autonomy and authority of parents and gives families choice in the ways they meet their child care needs. For child care advocates, however, it is inadequate both in vision and financial commitment. They argue that, even before tax, $100 a month is clearly insufficient to support the costs of regulated day care for young children. If anything, it provides only symbolic recognition of the unpaid care work of women and intimate family networks. In fact, it may reinforce traditional gendered biographies and, as already noted, traditional family forms.

Proponents of the UCCB applaud this social care policy as the embodiment of choice — providing choice to parents to rear their children as they see fit and to choose the kind of child care they want — formal or informal, public or private. In other words, this and similar measures are usually advanced through the gender-neutral language of *choice*. However, as Kershaw (2005: 929–930) rightly argues, this language is not gender neutral. The language of choice elevates the goal of individual liberty — the right to choose — over all other goals, including gender equality. It prioritizes "consumer sovereignty" and gives the illusion that a broad range of options is available for working parents. With dual-earner families increasingly becoming the norm, few families can choose to have one parent stay at home to care for a child, especially if the subsidies for child care are unrealistically low. Clearly, as well, single earner families do not have this choice. Instead, inadequate child care subsidies are more likely to underwrite part-time and precarious employment for women, as families struggle to make ends meet and care for their children. These so-called choices are neither equal nor universal (Kershaw 2004: 929–930).

The Social Union Framework Agreement and the Canada Social Transfer

As the above discussion underlines, the past decade has been marked by significant changes in the goals, funding, and governance of Canadian social policy. After abandoning cost-sharing arrangements in social assistance, the federal government has increasingly relied on two policy instruments to pursue its social policy objectives: tax credits and refunds and federal-provincial/territorial agreements that involve earmarked or "designated" (although not conditional) increases to the CHST (Noel 2003; Caledon Institute 2003). Many of these changes have been the result of federal unilateral action or supposedly one-time accommodations of the appeals of sub-national governments for more federal funds, especially to support growing health care costs. The federal government bolstered the CHST to support health care three times since the introduction of this block fund in 1994. In 2003, the CHST was divided into two separate block funds: the Canada Health Transfer and the Canada Social Transfer.

Reflecting the recommendations of the final report of the Commission on the Future of Health Care in Canada (the Romanow Report), as well as accords struck with the provinces and territories, the CHST was divided on an approximately 60/40 basis, with 60% of the federal transfer directed to the CHT and 40% into the CST. Unlike the CHT, which continues to be structured by the conditions of the *Canada Health Act*, there has been no clear articulation of the principles or policy goals underlying the CST. Although social policy advocates have attempted to generate a national debate about the policy goals and standards that should be applied to the new block grant, the CST puts no conditions on how the provinces actually spend these funds (CCSD 2004). As a block fund, it is fully fungible. After being transferred into the consolidated revenue funds of sub-national governments, there is no way of tracking whether it is actually spent on social policy objectives (Caledon Institute 2003: 2). This is a significant flaw in the current system of fiscal federalism.

In recent years, the provinces, beginning with Quebec, have argued that the current configuration of fiscal federalism needs to be corrected to remedy what is popularly termed as "fiscal imbalance" — a shortfall in revenue-raising capacity relative to spending responsibility. The issue of fiscal imbalance is not new in the history of Confederation. By its original design, the *British North America Act* (1867) gave the preponderance of revenue-raising capacity to the federal government and the bulk of responsibility for the social field — areas then considered to be "local" in nature — to the provinces. The issue of fiscal imbalance grew to be especially critical during the Great Depression of the 1930s when provincial resources proved inadequate in meeting the costs of mass unemployment and crises in the agricultural sector grounded in mortgage foreclosures, crop failures, and collapsed international commodity markets. This earlier debate about fiscal imbalance was largely resolved, in the early post-war years, through the implementation of national social programs, federal-provincial cost-sharing, and equalization.

The current charge of fiscal imbalance grows out of cuts to federal transfers to the provinces in the mid-1990s, the implementation of the CHST, and growing pressures on provincial social spending, especially in health care. At the same time, the capacity of the provinces to raise revenue has grown significantly in the past half century. They also have expressed growing reluctance to enter into either new national social programs or cost-sharing agreements with the federal government. They have done so, in part, because these programs may not completely align with provincial (and territorial) priorities and, in part, because of fear that the federal government might, in the future, unilaterally withdraw from its cost-sharing commitments, as was the case with CAP. However, questions, both of whether there now exists a fiscal imbalance and how to remediate it, are open to debate. For example, Mackenzie has demonstrated that interprovincial tax competition, rather than cuts to federal transfers, accounts for the appearance of fiscal imbalance. He thus argues that the current fiscal imbalance is "largely a problem inflicted by the provinces on themselves through tax competition" (2006:3). It is not immediately obvious, therefore, that additional tax room or larger unconditional federal cash transfers to the provinces and territories would alleviate the very real fiscal pressures on sub-national governments or enhance social programs for all Canadians. There are no mechanisms to ensure that additional tax room or cash transfers would, in fact, be directed to designated social programs or social goals.

Although we return to the issues of national standards, transparency and accountability in the social policy field in Part 6 of this report, the current debate about fiscal imbalance has not adequately engaged with these critical issues. This silence with respect to national standards and accountability in social policy stands in stark contrast to the principles and commitments contained in the SUFA, which was designed and endorsed by the federal and provincial/territorial governments (excluding Quebec) in 1999. The SUFA finds its roots in the federal government's unilateral and abrupt withdrawal from social assistance cost-sharing and its announced intention to curtail cash transfers for social programs with the introduction of the CHST in the 1995 federal budget.

In response, the provinces and territories, concerned both about the adequacy and stability of social program funding, quickly established the Ministerial Council on Social Policy Renewal to try to establish new ground rules for the creation and financing of social programs in Canada. After months of negotiation, a proposal began to take shape at the 1998 premiers' conference — the so-called Saskatoon Consensus — and again in Victoria the following year. While an underlying motivation for the SUFA was to increase federal funding for health care, the agreement forged a new intergovernmental agreement about the necessity of prior consultation and agreement among levels of government with respect to both changes in existing arrangements and the introduction of new national programs. As Noel et al. (2003: 3) explained:

The 1999 Social Union Framework Agreement was meant to provide common guiding principles and a "code of conduct" to manage the interaction between the two orders of government in health care, post-secondary education, training, social assistance, and social services. The stated objectives were to help governments work jointly to address the needs of Canadians; ensure adequate, stable and sustainable funding for social programs; prevent overlap and duplication; avoid and resolve intergovernmental disputes; and enhance public accountability and transparency.

Although the SUFA primarily set out new rules of the game with respect to the management of the social policy field between the two levels of government, it was also much more than this. Importantly, the intergovernmental agreement outlines a series of principles intended to guide social policy development and goals in the new millennium. These first principles include guidelines for the goals, substance, and process of social policy making. The SUFA affirms the following goals:

- Canada's social union should reflect and give expression to the fundamental values of Canadians: equality, respect for diversity, fairness, individual dignity and responsibility, and mutual aid and our responsibilities for one another.

- The social union must respect the equality, rights, and dignity of all Canadian women and men and their diverse needs.

- It must provide appropriate assistance for those in need.

- The social union needs to promote the full and active participation of all Canadians in Canada's social and economic life.

With respect to process, the two levels of government undertake to:

- work in partnership with individuals, families, communities, voluntary organizations, business and labour, and ensure appropriate opportunities for Canadians to have meaningful input into social policies and programs;

- monitor and measure outcomes of social programs and report regularly to constituents on the performance of these programs;

- share information and best practices to support the development of outcome measures, and work with other governments to develop, over time, comparable indicators to measure progress on agreed objectives;

- use funds transferred from another order of government for the purposes agreed and pass on increases to its residents; and

- ensure effective mechanisms for Canadians to participate in developing social priorities and reviewing outcomes.

Students of intergovernmental relations largely concur that the SUFA has failed to live up to its rhetoric and its potential. For example, while there has been some intergovernmental collaboration with respect to child-centred social policy, the federal government continues to act unilaterally in the social policy field and through the secrecy of the budgetary process (Noel 2003: 54–55). Similarly, Canada's governments have not opened the social policy field to public consultations, developed indicators or social audits, or shared best practices in any systematic or transparent way (Phillips 2003). As important, Canadians are largely unaware of the SUFA or that it commits their governments to respect the equality, rights, and dignity of all Canadians, as well as to provide appropriate levels of social assistance to those in need. The SUFA, for the most part, has been relegated to the sidelines of social policy development in Canada, but, as argued in the final section of this report, this need not be the case. The SUFA does commit Canadian governments to shape social policies around the goals of equality, including gender equality, and it does require governments to measure and monitor progress toward this goal.

The SUFA, in other words, does provide a framework to begin to address the erosion and fragmentation of Canada's social architecture. If Canadian governments have failed to make any significant progress toward broader social equity goals during the past decade, the source of this failure is not found in the SUFA or, for that matter, current instruments of fiscal federalism, but instead in a lack of vision and political will.

Three

Fragmentation and Erosion

WHEN THE FEDERAL government introduced the CHST in its 1995 budget, anti-poverty advocates and women's groups immediately rang the alarm bells, arguing that the elimination of CAP would hurt poor Canadians, and especially poor women and children who depend on provincial social assistance programs for their daily survival. The Canada Assistance Plan required the provinces to provide social assistance to all those in need, without work requirements or time limits, and with the right to appeal. Concern was immediately expressed that, within the context of a block grant, declining federal cash transfers, and the absence of conditions, the provinces would cut welfare benefits, impose punitive conditions for the receipt of welfare, and, drawing on the example of welfare reform in many American states, attempt to reduce welfare assistance rolls to a minimum.

Others contended that the block grant would enable provinces to shift funds away from social assistance to escalating health care costs or to tax cuts — two options that were far more popular with provincial electorates. Concern also was raised, to the limited extent that CAP set national standards for social assistance, that these would be lost and Canada's social assistance architecture would be fragmented into 13 different provincial and territorial welfare regimes, thus creating horizontal inequalities among Canadians, depending on where they lived. The only condition that the CHST explicitly placed on the provinces was that they could not put residency requirements on those in need of social assistance. Yet this minimal requirement also had potentially perverse effects for Canada's poor. It effectively discouraged any one province from augmenting its social assistance programs, because this might attract those in need from other provincial jurisdictions with less generous welfare regimes.

Over the course of the last decade, Canada's social assistance regime has experienced a remarkable degree of fragmentation and erosion. It would be incorrect, however, to assume that these outcomes are due solely either to the introduction of the CHST or to the reactions of the provinces. As already noted, the CHST was an enabling instrument that facilitated these outcomes, but the fragmentation and erosion of social assistance in Canada must be understood as a matter of political choice, at both the federal and provincial levels of government. Responding to peaks in welfare rolls in the early 1990s, many provinces already had begun to tighten eligibility requirements, reduce benefits, and attempt to shift the poor from social assistance into the labour force (Jenson 2003: vi). Equally important, despite all the rhetoric about ending child poverty in Canada, federal social policy during the past decade has had a negligible impact on poverty rates and, indeed, may have indirectly contributed to the steep drop in the incomes and purchasing power of the most vulnerable groups, such as sole mothers.

Although there is some debate about how best to understand and measure poverty, Statistics Canada's Low Income Cut-Off (LICO) is usually employed as an approximate measure of the incidence and depth of poverty in Canada (Kunz and Frank 2004). According to this measure (after tax), about 2.7 million Canadians, 54% of them women, lived in poverty in 2003. Moreover, Canadian women are more likely than men to live in deep poverty and for longer periods (Townson 2005: 2). Gender-disaggregated data, however, mask the fact that, while poverty is gendered across virtually all social categories, women's poverty tends to be concentrated in identifiable groups. According to 2001 Census data on before-tax income, fully 36% of Aboriginal women live in poverty (compared to 17% of non-Aboriginal women), as do 29% of visible minority women, 35% of recent women immigrants (arriving between 1991 and 2000), and 26% of women with disabilities (Townson 2005: 2–3).

Among female one-parent families, a category that cuts across all of these groups, poverty rates are even higher. According to Townson (2005: 2), the after-tax low-income rate for female one-parent families was 38% in 2003, down slightly from 39% in 2002. This compares to a 2003 rate of about 13% among lone-parent families headed by men and 7% among two-parent families with children. In 2001, single-parent mothers accounted for 85% of all single-parent families in Canada. and over 90% of all poor single-parent families (NCW 2001: 14).

The feminization of poverty persists even though Canadian women, including those with young children, are increasingly entering the paid labour force. The employment rate for women increased from 42% in 1972 to 57% in 2003. Numerous factors underlie the gendered and racialized face of poverty in Canada. Apart from the ongoing legacy of sexism, colonialism and racism, women both in full- and part-time work — as well as women across all age groups — consistently earn less than their male counterparts. Overall, the earnings of women in paid employment (both full- and part-time combined) average 64% of the average earnings of men (Townson 2005: 4). This can partly be attributed to the continuing concentration of women workers in the characteristically low-paid service and retail sectors. Related to this, women are more likely to be "precariously" employed in part-time, limited-term, contractual, and non-standard work, not the least because of the constraints of ongoing child care and family responsibilities. In addition to this, immigrant women often find it difficult to have their educational and professional credentials recognized by Canadian employers, and thus are forced into unemployment or underemployment.

None of these factors is particularly new, and the negative impacts of each could be lessened through public policies such as minimum wage legislation and accessible and affordable child care. According to a study released by the Law Commission of Canada in 2005, entitled *Is Work*

Working?, in 2000, almost two million adult Canadian workers earned less than $10 an hour. Some 670,000 of these, mostly women, attempted to sole-support their families on less than $10 an hour. The study underlines that existing laws and policies still assume that "someone," other than the worker, provides the child, elder and home care for the worker when, in reality, Canadian workers increasingly struggle to balance the demands of work and family with little public support.

During the past decade, Canadian governments have had a dubious record with respect to poverty reduction, as well as its gendered underpinnings. For almost two decades, Canadians have witnessed a sustained erosion of social spending. Although federal cutbacks were initially justified in terms of containing growing deficits, social spending has been only marginally enhanced with the return of large budgetary surpluses in the late 1990s. As Yalnizyan (2005c: 216) reported, federal spending as a share of the economy shrank dramatically since the mid-1990s, from 16% of the gross domestic product (GDP) in 1994 to 11% in 2001, and is projected to remain around 11.6% until 2010. Federal spending as a share of the GDP has not been this low since before Canada's post-war social architecture was set in place in the late 1940s, and is well below Canada's average spending-to-GDP ratio since 1946 of 15.3%. As a result, Canada increasingly appears as a "social laggard" among developed countries. In 2001, for example, Canada ranked 25th among 30 OECD countries in public social expenditures (as a percentage of GDP). While only four of the 30 OECD countries have higher national incomes per capita, Canada ranks 11th with respect to child poverty and 12th on the relative poverty scale.

Government spending priorities represent a complex mixture of precedent, need, political pressure and influence, social values, and political will. The ways in which governments spend budgetary surpluses, perhaps better than any other indicator, provides a rough measure of both political influence and political will. From this perspective, the federal government's allocation of successive and large budgetary surpluses since 1998 demonstrates that poverty reduction and gender equality are no longer governmental priorities. As shown in Table 3, the vast weight

TABLE 3 *New Federal Spending Initiatives 1997–98 to 2003–04*

Tax Cuts	$152 ($15 billion in CCTB)
Debt reduction	$61 billion
CHST	$34 billion ($2.2 billion for ECDE)
EI parental leave	$3 billion
Departmental	$42 billion ($11.6 billion to Defence; $24.8 billion to Canada Opportunities Strategy)

Source Yalnizyan (2005a: 94).

of the federal surplus has been directed to tax reduction, which tends to benefit the corporate sector and higher income earners, and debt reduction. Key federal initiatives, such as the national children's agenda and parental leave, represent only a fraction of new federal spending. As well, the large cuts exacted to programs for Canada's poor, and to government departments and agencies responsible for developing and administering social policy, have not been restored to previous levels.

Yalnizyan (2005a: 79) argued that, "at the start of the surplus era, the federal government was faced with a critical choice: it could reinvest in the social programming that had been cut so deeply in the deficit era; or it could redirect resources to tax-based incentives and expenditures." As already noted, the federal government selected the latter, contributing to a growing trend toward the fiscalization of social policy. Fiscalization means social policy goals are pursued only indirectly through the tax system and the spending priorities of families, while taxable income determines both who is eligible for support and the level of support attained. Some argue that fiscalization is a preferable way to provide income support for the poor, because it is a private mechanism that avoids stigmatizing the poor. As well, fiscalization allows the federal government to provide income support directly to individuals and families, enabling it to bypass the provinces and take full political credit for the program. In the increasingly competitive atmosphere of federal–provincial relations, these two factors are undoubtedly enticing for federal policy makers.

However, fiscalization, at best, is an indirect social policy instrument that is both precarious and lacks transparency. Benefits provided through tax expenditures can be increased, decreased, targeted or eliminated with one stroke of the finance minister's pen behind the veiled secrecy of the budget process and without debate about best practices or the consequences for Canadian families (Noel 2003). Finally, tax expenditures do not necessarily directly attend to the policy goal for which they are intended. As in the case of the CCTB, for example, marginal increases in family income do not necessarily provide more security, opportunity, or equality for Canada's poor children.

More important for our purposes, tax expenditures are not gender neutral. Lisa Philipps (2006) has argued that these "tax-delivered social policies" have two systemic disadvantages for many women. First, tax-based measures generally do not benefit low-income women because these women do not have enough taxable income or tax liability to claim deductions, exemptions or credits. More women than men in Canada live on low incomes. In 2003, for example, the average income of the 208,000 women who headed lone-parent families was a shocking $6,300 below the poverty line (Townson 2005: 2–4). Table 4 underlines the alarming picture of women's overrepresentation in the lowest income groups. Women with incomes of less than $10,000 account for 30% of all women who file taxes (versus 18.4% of men) (Yalnizyan 2005b: 11).

The Caregiver Tax Credit, introduced in 1998, provides a clear example of how tax expenditures can and do rule out many women from benefiting from a program simply because it is tied to taxable income. Philipps (1999) explained that the government presented the caregiver credit as a way of recognizing the value of women's unpaid caregiving work. However, the credit can only be claimed against tax otherwise payable. This excludes many primary caregivers with little or no income and explains why men receive about 60% of caregiver credits. Philipps also noted that tax deductions and exemptions do not equally benefit women since the value of deductions and exemptions rises with a taxpayers' marginal rate, and women are far more likely to be at the bottom end of income earners. Measures such as tax deductions and tax sheltering through Retirement Savings Plans (RSPs) and Registered Retirement Savings Plans (RRSPs) favour men heavily. Men received over 60% of tax savings from RSP deductions in 2002 and almost 70% from RRSP deductions. Hence proposed increases to RRSP limits, such as those announced in the 2005 budget, benefit a small proportion of people earning over $100,000. According to Yalnizyan (2005b: 11): "Only 1% of all female tax filers — about 145,000 women — are in an income category that could gain from the new savings limits. About 550,000 men, or about 5% of male tax-filers, could benefit from these increases." Although the Harper government has enhanced caregiver tax credits, the gender biases in the very design of the policy remain unchallenged.

A second gender bias related to tax expenditures is that they trust that the primary breadwinner will share these gains with the household. This ignores a good deal of evidence about intra-household financial inequalities, assumes caregivers are in a spousal/partner relationship, and leaves out those where neither partner earns sufficient taxable income to benefit from the credit (Philipps 2006). This male breadwinner bias of tax-delivered social policies structures any claims on the state for social benefits around the norm of full-time, lifelong participation in the labour force, and assumes that a wage paid to the male breadwinner provides for the cash needs of dependants, leaving women with little or no autonomy of decision making and control (Elson and Cagatay 2000: 1355). Tax expenditures extended to the family also tend to mask what Lister (2004: 56) called feminized "hidden poverty" within families. Sociologists have long demonstrated that neither income nor consumption is evenly distributed within families when family incomes increase. Instead, women are more likely to sacrifice for other family members, especially for their children.

The Canadian Child Tax Benefit, the most significant tax-delivered social policy introduced in the past decade, has improved the purchasing power of increasingly greater numbers of low- and middle-income Canadian families. Similar to the American federal government's Earned Income Tax Credit (EITC), or the United Kingdom's Working Families Tax Credit, the CCTB aims to increase the purchasing power of families

TABLE 4 *Who Benefits? The Distribution of Tax Filers*

	Men	Women	Total	Men	Women	Total
All tax filers	11,187,840	11,665,820	22,853,660	100	100	100
Taxable	8,423,180	7,092,990	15,516,170	75	61	68
Non-taxable	2,764,650	4,572,830	7,337,480	25	39	32
All tax filers						
Under $10,000	2,056,030	3,467,500	5,523,530	18.4	29.7	24.2
Less than $15,000	3,127,550	3,833,390	6,960,940	28.0	32.9	30.5
Less than $20,000	4,059,500	4,411,350	8,470,850	36.3	37.8	37.1
Less than $25,000	4,884,280	5,001,350	9,885,630	43.7	42.9	43.3
Less than $30,000	5,688,050	5,706,390	11,394,440	50.8	48.9	49.9
Over $100,000	548,130	144,480	692,610	4.9	1.2	3.0

Source CCRA (2004).

with children, especially the working poor. It is represented as a fiscal lever, which addresses the complex and multi-causal problem of child poverty. Yet, according to the federal government, this tax benefit also addresses women's equality. In 2005, then Minister of Finance Ralph Goodale indicated that the federal government considered the CCTB to be an initiative which demonstrated that the federal government takes "gender issues very seriously" and is committed to "the principles of gender equality."[6] This statement reveals a central assumption informing social policy change in the last decade: the feminization of poverty and broader gender equality goals can be subsumed under the categories of child poverty and child care. However, the proposition that "what is good for the child is good for the mother" is not borne out in poverty statistics. In fact, the reverse formulation is probably more accurate.

As many commentators have noted, the very design of the CCTB, and especially the NCBS, has had the unintended consequence of aggravating the poverty experienced by sole mothers on social assistance in Canada. As discussed above, the CCTB initiative allows provincial governments to claw back the NCBS from welfare families, with the understanding that these savings would be spent on additional supports and services for poor families. As of 2004, Prince Edward Island, Ontario,[7] Saskatchewan, British Columbia, and the three territories continued to exercise this option (NCW 2005: x).

The issues of whether and how provinces claw back the NCBS has further fragmented and complicated Canada's social assistance architecture. As the National Council of Welfare (2005: 15) argued, the clawback also "discriminates against welfare families, and especially single-parent families on welfare. Most poor single-parent families are headed by women, so the clawback also discriminates against women." According to the Council's estimates, 11% of the 1.3 million Canadian families eligible to receive the NCBS are denied this benefit, as well as 54.4% of families with children on welfare across Canada. The Council (2005: x) concluded that the "clawback and the current funding arrangements for welfare are blatant and long-standing examples of bad social policy, and bad social policy almost inevitably produces bad results."

The fragmentation and erosion of Canada's social assistance regime during the past decade also can be clearly tracked across the provinces and territories. Since the late-1980s, all the provinces have systematically cut away at their income and support programs of last resort without making any appreciable reinvestments to support Canada's poorest citizens. After a decade of social policy reform, social assistance rates have dropped dramatically to their lowest levels since the 1980s (after adjusting for inflation) and show little sign of abating. The National Council of Welfare (2005: ix) reported that, between 2003 and 2004, among the 52 calculations it makes with respect to welfare rates for different household types across 13 jurisdictions, fully 86% were lower than the year before.

The elimination of the minimal conditions attached to CAP effectively freed the provinces from the legislative requirement to provide assistance to those in need, regardless of category. Throughout the late 1990s, the provinces variously responded by reducing social assistance payments, especially for those categorized as "single employables," creating American-style work-for-welfare regimes, denying support to some and tightening eligibility for others, and reducing work exemption periods for new mothers (Rice and Prince 2004). By 2003, all of the provinces had adopted some form of "active welfare" model, which requires welfare recipients to engage in some form of paid or voluntary work, training program, or job search activity to qualify for social assistance (Jenson 2003).

Although Quebec experimented with a form of workfare in the 1980s, Alberta was a policy leader in the 1990s, embracing active welfare policies that aim to help "people to regain independence through employment and training" (NCW 2003: 71) or what others have termed "the shortest route to paid employment." Beginning in the fall of 1993, social assistance benefits were reduced by 13% for single parents and by 12% for couples with two children, and shelter allowances were reduced. The Supports for Independence (SFI) program required mandatory employment training, while recipients who either lived with a relative or in a common-law relationship or refused or quit work forfeited some or all of their benefits. Although those categorized as single employable adults felt the brunt of the cuts, policy for single parents was also changed, requiring this group to look for work or take up training once their youngest child was six months of age. At the same time, people with a disability were moved from welfare to a separate program called Assured Income for the Severely Handicapped (AISH), which has strict eligibility requirements (NCW 1997).

The Alberta government argued that these changes were necessary to "ensure that those on social assistance received a level of support not exceeding that earned by working Albertans" (Boessenkool 1997: 6). It is worth noting that, throughout this period, Alberta enforced a minimum wage which was well below the Canadian average. More recently, Alberta has redesigned its social assistance regime to put more emphasis on paving the shortest road to work. While the new *Income and Employment Supports Act*, or "Alberta Works," eliminates the SFI entitlements, it provides enhanced health coverage and child-support services for those in training programs. According to the minister responsible, the new program attempts to make "a direct link between social policy and labour policy" (Cryderman 2004: A7). Since the 1993 cuts, Alberta welfare rates have seen only one increase of approximately $20 a month (*Edmonton Journal* 2005: A18).

In 1995–96, Ontario's newly-elected Harris government quickly followed the Alberta example with a harsher social assistance regime more closely modelled after the Wisconsin welfare reform called "Wisconsin Works." Social assistance levels for all categories of recipients (except seniors and those with a disability) were cut by about 22%. Those in common-law relationships were deemed ineligible for social assistance, the spouse-in-the-house rule was reinstated, and "Ontario Works," a mandatory work-for-welfare scheme, was introduced. Social assistance recipients were required to engage in paid or voluntary work in order to receive and maintain benefits. Moreover, individuals in the workfare program were prohibited from unionizing to ensure minimally acceptable working conditions, even though, later in the decade, this restriction was deemed, by the United Nations, to be a violation of the UN Covenant on Economic, Social, and Cultural Rights (Bashevkin 2002: 84). After a decade, however, the mandatory work program has received very mixed reviews. Work for welfare programs have proven to be very costly and difficult to administer and evaluate with respect to best practices. There have been ongoing difficulties in finding paid work for those categorized as employable and thus many meet their hourly requirements by working as part-time or casual volunteers for business, government, or community organizations. Studies report that there is a very high unemployment rate (27%) among those pushed off of social assistance (Kitchen 2005).

British Columbia, following the examples of Alberta, Ontario, and selected American states, introduced Canada's most stringent social assistance regime in 2002. The B.C. *Employment and Assistance Act* cut the social assistance budget by approximately 25%, reduced benefits to single parents and employable individuals, varying by age, from $43 to as much as $98 a month, cut shelter, crisis, and child care allowances for the poor, enhanced its workfare component, eliminated earned income exemptions and — a first in Canada — introduced a time limit on the receipt of social assistance benefits. "Employable clients" over the age of 19 are limited to a total of 24 cumulative months of assistance within any five-year period (B.C. Employment and Assistance 2004). While this new regime effectively reduced the province's welfare rolls by 42% between 2001 and 2005, similar to other welfare-to-work programs in both Canada and the United States, the plan has hit a number of significant roadblocks. The program was revised in 2004 to increase the number of exemptions from the two year cut-off measure. Moreover, the government's 2005 review of the program found that it cost far more than expected ($10,770) to move a person from welfare to work, and failed to move people quickly into the paid labour force. Half of those trained for work under the program could not find jobs afterward. The program is being redesigned to contract out employment and job-training programs to private sector providers (Matas 2005: A6).

Many policy analysts argue that Canada's poverty rates remain high largely because of the changes in EI and provincial social assistance regimes that have been implemented in the past decade, leading to the well-grounded contention that Canadian governments fail the most vulnerable citizens (Rice 2002: 116). The proportion of Canadians receiving social assistance has dropped significantly in the past decade — nationally, from 10.4% in 1993 to 5.5% in 2003. The provinces registering the greatest reductions in the number of social assistance recipients during this decade were Alberta (-70.5%), New Brunswick[8] (-50.1%), Ontario (-47.6%), and British Columbia (-44.1%) (Roy 2004: 3.2). It is difficult to assess the degree to which these declines can be attributed to government programs or to a growing economy. The national economy tottered on the verge of a deep recession in the early 1990s when the provinces' welfare rolls peaked. At the same time, social assistance benefits remain inadequate considering that, in recent years, there has been both reduced demand for social assistance and healthy economic growth. To put it more bluntly, Canada's governments have more fiscal room to enhance social assistance benefits but, instead, they have actually decreased them, often dramatically.

Tables 5 and 6 tell part of this story, first for single parents who have tended to fare slightly better than other categories of social assistance recipients and, second, for all categories of welfare recipients. Table 5

TABLE 5 *Welfare Benefits in the Provinces and Territories, 1994–2004 (single-parent, one-child family, 2004 constant dollars)*

	Peak Year	1994	2004	% Change
Newfoundland and Labrador	1992	13,469	11,761	-13
Prince Edward Island	1986	12,635	10,077	-20
Nova Scotia	1989	12,630	9,217	-27
New Brunswick	1997	11,333	9,922	-12
Quebec	1994	13,788	10,910	-21
Ontario	1992	17,110	10,784	-37
Manitoba	1992	11,525	9,636	-16
Saskatchewan	1986	12,416	9,068	-27
Alberta	1986	10,994	8,784	-20
British Columbia	1994	14,309	10,311	-28
Yukon	1997	15,682	16,526	10
Northwest Territories	1993	22,920	18,291	-20
Nunavut	1999		18,392	

Source NCW (2005). Welfare incomes for 2004, calculated from tables 4.1 and 4.2.

shows the peak year for welfare benefits for a singe-parent, one-child family, indicating benefit levels for both 1994 and 2004 (in 2004 constant dollars), and the percentage across this decade. It shows that, for three of the 13 provincial and territorial jurisdictions, welfare benefits for single parents peaked after the introduction of the CHST. Moreover, in all jurisdictions save Yukon, welfare benefits have declined, in some cases quite significantly. In eight of the jurisdictions, the decline has been at or greater than 20%. Some of the most dramatic declines have been experienced in Canada's richest provinces: Ontario (-37%), British Columbia (-28%), and Alberta (-20%). The decline in welfare benefits for single parents in Alberta since its peak year in 1986 is about 61%.

Table 6, using 2001 data and total welfare income (including basic social assistance, additional benefits, the CCTB, provincial/territorial benefits, the federal GST credit and provincial tax credits) shows the adequa-

TABLE 6 *Canadian Welfare Incomes as a Percentage of the Poverty Line by Family Type and Province, 2001*

	Total Income $	Poverty Line $	Total Income as % of Poverty Line
Newfoundland and Labrador			
Single employable	3,276	16,167	20
Person with a disability	8,902	16,167	55
Single parent, One child	14,670	20,209	73
Couple, two children	17,474	30,424	57
Prince Edward Island			
Single employable	5,846	16,055	36
Person with a disability	8,772	16,055	55
Single parent, one child	12,530	20,070	62
Couple, two children	19,399	30,214	64
Nova Scotia			
Single employable	4,817	16,167	30
Person with a disability	8,312	16,167	51
Single parent, one child	12,250	20,209	61
Couple, two children	18,353	30,424	60
New Brunswick			
Single employable	3,374	16,167	21
Person with a disability	6,902	16,167	43
Single parent, one child	12,888	20,209	64
Couple, two children	16,206	30,424	53
Quebec			
Single employable	6,415	18,849	34
Person with a disability	9,314	18,849	49
Single parent, one child	13,318	23,561	57
Couple, two children	16,919	35,471	48

	Total Income $	Poverty Line $	Total Income as % of Poverty Line
Ontario			
Single employable	6,829	18,849	36
Person with a disability	11,763	18,849	62
Single parent, one child	13,828	23,561	59
Couple, two children	18,330	35,471	52
Manitoba			
Single employable	5,558	18,849	29
Person with a disability	8,352	18,849	44
Single parent, one child	12,330	23,561	52
Couple, two children	17,725	35,471	50
Saskatchewan			
Single employable	5,978	16,167	37
Person with a disability	8,662	16,167	54
Single parent, one child	12,367	20,209	61
Couple, two children	18,210	30,424	60
Alberta			
Single employable	5,030	18,849	27
Person with a disability	7,596	18,849	40
Single parent, one child	11,619	23,561	49
Couple, two children	18,395	35,471	52
British Columbia			
Single employable	6,457	18,849	34
Person with a disability	9,782	18,849	52
Single parent, one child	14,069	23,561	60
Couple, two children	18,412	35,471	52

Note "Total welfare income" includes all income from basic social assistance, additional benefits, the Canada Child Tax Benefit, provincial/territorial child benefits, the federal Goods and Services Tax (GST) credit, and provincial/territorial tax credits.
Source Prepared by the Canadian Council on Social Development, using NCW (2002).

cy of welfare benefits as a percentage of the poverty line. For single employables, the range is between 20% of the poverty line in Newfoundland and Labrador to 37% of the poverty line in Saskatchewan. Benefits for persons with a disability have settled around 50% of the poverty line for all provinces except Ontario. Benefits for single parents range from 73% of the poverty line in Newfoundland and Labrador to a low of 49% in Alberta. Finally, the range for couples with children ranges from 48% in Quebec to 64% of the poverty line in Prince Edward Island. These data underline the fragmentation, erosion, and inadequacy of social assistance rates across Canada.

While it is impossible to review the diversity of provincial and territorial social policy initiatives that have been adopted by the provinces since the introduction of the CHST, a few generalizations are warranted. First, all the provinces now frame the goals of their social assistance policies in terms of getting people off welfare and into the paid labour force, even if employment is in dead-end jobs that are unlikely to lift people out of poverty (Jenson 2003: 35). Second, the broader principles of social citizenship, poverty eradication, and social inclusion are almost entirely absent as motivating principles for provincial and territorial social policy reform during the past decade, with the possible exception of Quebec. Early in the new millennium, the Quebec National Assembly unanimously adopted Bill 112, a national strategy to combat poverty and social exclusion. Unique in North America, the Bill's preamble expresses "the desire of Quebec society as a whole to act in a coordinated manner and pursue a course of action designed to combat poverty and social exclusion."[9] The initiative identifies poverty as an obstacle to the protection of and respect for human dignity. Yet the striking feature about this law, as well as all federal and provincial social policy reform over the past decade, is the systematic erasure of gender both in rhetoric and substance. As this report makes clear, poverty and low income in Canada are decidedly, systemically, invariably gendered. Lister (2004: 55) underlined the point that "gender constitutes the most profound differentiating division: a gendered analysis of poverty reveals not simply its unequal incidence, but also that both cause and effect are deeply gendered. The conceptual and methodological implications go well beyond adding women in."

Of all the shifts in Canada's social policy regime in the past decade, the erasure of gender, gender differences, and differences within gendered categories is perhaps the most pronounced and inexplicable. This erasure helps account for persistent differences among men and women and among women themselves with respect to poverty, income, and life chances. This inattention to gender also helps account for the failure of successive governments to crack the problem of child poverty in Canada. Poor children live in poor families, disproportionately in female-headed, sole-parent families. Tax benefits for children "neglect the fact that female labour force participation is inextricably linked both to women's role as primary caregiver and the burden of unpaid labour. It is also linked to structural barriers within the paid labour market, such as discrimination and occupational segregation" (Paterson et al. 2004: 139). As Vosko (2002: 189) rightly observed of recent social policy reform, "the absence of gendered provisions does not amount to gender-neutral consequences." In the next chapter, we explore the factors underpinning the disappearance of the gendered subject in Canadian social policy reform.

Four

Gender-Based Policy Capacity

IN THE PAST 30 years, Canadians have witnessed both a marked rise and precipitous decline in the importance attributed to gender in the development of social policy and in the pursuit of the broader social goals of gender equality and inclusive citizenship. Although gender continues to be a central factor informing policy development among international institutions, such as the United Nations, various international development agencies and, to a lesser extent, the European Union, it has progressively fallen off the political radar in many Western democracies. This is especially the case in Anglo-American democracies, such as Canada and Australia, where neoliberal governing assumptions have been embraced. During the past decade, the discourses and strategies associated with the policy goal of achieving gender equality have been systematically displaced through the prioritization of child- and family-centred initiatives, market principles, and individual self-reliance (Brodie 2002). The combined effect of these new currents in social policy thinking, as Anne Summers (2003: 6), a former head of the Australian Office of the Status of Women, has observed, suggests that "we have come to the end of equality."

The progressive erasure of gender as a fundamental variable in both the conceptualization and implementation of social policy has been attributed to many diverse factors, among them the apparent cyclical nature of the women's movement, the ascendancy of market thinking inside of government, the institutionalization of the women's movement, the fragmentation of the women's movement, a backlash against feminism, and the rise of social conservatism (Sawer 2006). Although each of these broader social changes has obvious implications for the political currency of gender, this chapter largely focuses on the forces impacting on the capacities of gender-based policy machinery, within the federal government and in the provinces, to influence social policy development and implementation.

The development of gender-based policy units within the Canadian federal government has a long history, dating back to the establishment of the Women's Bureau within the Ministry of Labour in 1954. Following the lead of the International Labour Organization (ILO), the Women's Bureau tracked women's participation in the paid labour force and was instrumental in the development of equal pay legislation in 1956 and maternity leave legislation in 1971 (Burt and Hardman 2001: 201–202). During these early years, Saskatchewan also established a women's bureau with its labour ministry. As Table 7 demonstrates, however, federal gender-based policy machinery became more elaborate during two periods: first in the early-1970s and again in the mid-1990s. During both periods, Canadian institutional capacity building corresponded to and interacted with key gender-based initiatives undertaken by the United Nations, especially those arising from the UN International Decade of Women (1975–85) and the Beijing Platform for Action (1995).

In the early-1970s, Canada emerged as a leader among developed countries in the development of policies and agencies designed to enhance the status of women in all sectors of society, and provide them with points of entry into the policy-making process. The 1970 Report of the Royal Commission on the Status of Women (RCSW) was instrumental to this process. The idea of establishing such a commission had been pushed by a national coalition of women's groups during the 1960s, especially after a similar task force was appointed in the United States by the Kennedy administration. In 1966, the Pearson government appointed journalist Florence Bird to head a Royal Commission and directed it to "recommend what steps might be taken by the federal government to ensure for women equal opportunities with men in all aspects of Canadian society" (Canada 1970: vii). In all, the Commission made 167 recommendations, some 122 of which were exclusively federal responsibilities. The RCSW is widely recognized as having set much of the political and legislative agenda for the Canadian women's movement for the 1970s and beyond (Brodie 1995: 42–44).

One of the most immediate impacts of the Royal Commission was the elaboration of a network of gender-based policy machinery within the federal government — one of the most elaborate in the world at the time (See Table 7). In 1971, the Office of the Coordinator for the Status of Women was established within the Privy Council Office, and a year later the Women's Program was set up within the Citizenship Branch of the Secretary of State. Its mandate was "the development of a society in which the full potential of women as citizens is recognized and utilized" (Burt 1994: 216). This mandate reflected the prevailing governing philosophy at the time that state funding of disadvantaged groups enriched both Canadian democracy and the public policy process by making it more responsive to community needs and priorities. Guided by this commitment, federal funding for the Women's Program grew from a meagre $233,000 in 1973 to $12.4 million in 1987, leaving in its wake a mosaic of national feminist organizations with the resources to generate research on women's issues, lobby government and hold it accountable, as well as a vibrant mix of grassroots women's organizations that provided education, shelters and services to women marginalized by, for example, abuse, immigrant status and poverty (Burt and Hardman 2001: 204). In 1973, this gender-based infrastructure was further developed with the establishment of the Canadian Advisory Council on the Status of Women (CACSW), an arm's-length organization designed to provide policy advice to the federal government and to liaise with the organized women's movement. In 1976, the Office of the Coordinator was moved

TABLE 7 *Building Federal Gender-Based Policy Machinery*

1954	Women's Bureau (Department of Labour)
1970	Royal Commission on the Status of Women
1971	Office of Coordinator for Status of Women (Privy Council Office)
1972	Women's Program (Secretary of State)
1973	Canadian Advisory Council on the Status of Women (CACSW)
1976	Status of Women Canada
	Minister Responsible for the Status of Women
1993	Women's Bureau moved (to Strategic Policy Branch HRDC)
1995	Canada commits to Bejiing Platform
	CACSW disbanded
	Women's Program Integrated into Status of Women Canada
	Minister of State Responsible for the Status of Women downgraded to Secretary of State
1996	*Setting the Stage for the Next Century: The Federal Plan for Gender Equity*
1998–	Office of Senior Advisor on Aboriginal Women's Issues and Gender Equality
	International Women's Equity Section (Foreign Affairs and International Trade)
	Gender Equality Division (Canadian International Development Agency)
	Women's Health Bureau (Health Canada)

Sources SWC (2002: 8–13); Burt and Hardman (2001: 201–222).

out of the Privy Council Office and expanded into an interdepartmental co-ordinating agency — Status of Women Canada — and linked into the federal cabinet through the creation of a Minister Responsible for the Status of Women.

By 1975, International Women's Year, the Canadian federal government had already built up the national machinery to advocate for women's equality within government, something the UN Plan for Action for the UN Decade of Women had called on member states to do. Indeed, by the end of the decade, about two-thirds of UN member states established their own national machineries, many of which emulated the models already provided by such leader countries as Canada and Australia (Sawer 2006). Canada's "feminist state" had built within it:

- organizations designated, in contemporary terminology, to build "gender-based social capital," that is, to empower civil society groups to educate, provide services and make their demands known to government (through the Women's Program);

- an autonomous agency designed to link academic, provincial, and community policy networks to the federal government, to advocate on women's issues and provide policy advice (through the CACSW); and

- an interdepartmental agency within the federal bureaucracy to co-ordinate policy initiatives (Status of Women) and inform the Minister Responsible for the Status of Women who held a seat at the cabinet table.

During these years, many Canadian provinces also followed the federal example and set up some form of gender-based policy machinery or advisory mechanism. Because the history of these organizations is not well documented, it is difficult to provide a comprehensive account of gender-based policy capacity at the provincial level. Table 8 provides an overview of the origins and current status of these organizations, based on documents, web searches, and telephone interviews with provincial officials (see Appendix C). It shows that, by the mid-1980s, most provinces had two, if not three, vehicles for policy advice. First, most provinces had some form of advisory council, which generally was created through provincial legislation, consisting of appointees supported by permanent employees or civil servants, and funded by government (in the

TABLE 8 *Provincial Gender-Based Policy Machinery*

Alberta	The Alberta Advisory Council on Women's Issues, established in 1986 and officially dissolved, through sunset legislation, in 1996.
British Columbia	The Ministry of Women's Equality, first and only free-standing Canadian department for gender equality, established in 1993 and dissolved in 2001, replaced by Women's Equality and Social Programs Branch, a sub-unit of Ministry of Community, Aboriginal, and Women's Services.
Manitoba	The Manitoba Advisory Council established in 1982, formalized in legislation in 1987, and renamed as Manitoba Women's Advisory Council in 1991. Most recently, the Advisory Council has established a semi-autonomous connection to Manitoba Women's Directorate (established in 1984), reporting through the Directorate to the Minister for the Status of Women.
New Brunswick	The Women's Issues Branch in Executive Council Office as well as New Brunswick Advisory Council on the Status of Women, which was created and is funded by the provincial government.
Newfoundland and Labrador	The Provincial Advisory Council on the Status of Women, established in 1980, funded by and reporting annually to the House of Assembly as well as the Women's Policy Office, housed within the Executive Council with the Assistant Deputy Minister on Women's Policy reporting to the Minister Responsible for the Status of Women.
Nova Scotia	The Nova Scotia Advisory Council on the Status of Women merged with the Women's Directorate, a provincial agency, in 1996. The Women's Directorate was created in 1988 and reports to the Minister Responsible for the Status of Women.

Ontario	The Ontario Council on the Status of Women was established in 1973, dissolved in 1995, and replaced by the Ontario Advisory Council on Women's Issues in 1996. The Ontario Women's Directorate, housed in the Office of the Premier, was established in 1983. In 1995, the Directorate was substantially reduced and its focus narrowed to advancing women's economic equality and preventing violence against women. Ontario also has had a women's bureau within the Ministry of Labour.
Prince Edward Island	The Prince Edward Advisory Council was established in 1975 through an order-in-council and received full legislative standing in 1988 through the PEI Advisory Council on the Status of Women Act. The Council consists of non-salaried appointed members and a small permanent staff that meets with the Minister Responsible for the Status of Women. Prince Edward Island also has the Interministerial Women's Secretariat with a small permanent staff.
Quebec	The Secretariat à la condition féminine, established in 1973, consists of council members, appointed on the basis of recommendations of women's groups and a permanent staff. It has a head and regional offices and reports to the Ministère du Conseil Executive.
Saskatchewan	The Saskatchewan Advisory Council on the Status of Women, established in 1974, was autonomous and government funded. The Women's Division in the Department of Labour, was established in 1963, and renamed the Women's Bureau in 1966. The 1983 *Women's Secretariat Act*, established Secretariat to provide research and policy support to the Minister Responsible for the Status of Women. It was merged with the new Department of Human Resources in 1987 and renamed the Women's Directorate. In 2002, the Status of Women Office was created within the Department of Labour and has a small staff that reports to the Minister of Labour. Saskatchewan also has the Intragovernmental Committee of Advisors on Women's Policy.

earlier years, both provincial and federal). These advisory mechanisms predominantly reported either to the provincial executive office or to a minister responsible for the status of women. The table also shows that most provinces, especially during the 1980s, developed policy machinery inside of provincial bureaucracies in the form of a women's bureau, directorate, or secretariat. British Columbia was unique in Canada, however, by establishing a line department, the Ministry of Women's Equality, in 1993. A self-standing gender-focused ministry is generally considered to be an optimal organizational strategy to pursue gender-equality goals (Sawer 2006).

In these early years, Canada's gender-based policy machinery ranked high on practitioner and academic assessments of best practices with respect to advancing gender equality within government. For the most part, gender units were:

- *centrally located* in an interdepartmental agency as well as in key departments and able to monitor the gender impacts of all kinds of policies;

- *backed by authority*, fortified by the Royal Commission report, and able to draw on the influence first of the Privy Council Office and then of cabinet and, at the provincial level, the premier's office or executive council;

- *goal congruent* with broader governing philosophy of citizenship equality and inclusiveness; and

- *organizationally linked* to community groups and the growing second wave of the Canadian women's movement, nationally and provincially (Sawer 2006; Teghtsoonian 2004; Summers 2003).

However, almost as quickly as this policy infrastructure was set in place, broader social and political forces began to erode both the resources afforded these units to build community alliances and influence government actors, and the very saliency attributed to gender and gender equality in the policy-making process. In the current era, both the gendered focus of social policy and the broad social goal of advancing gender equality have been virtually erased from the policy agendas of Canada's governments. The disappearance of women both as a focus of public policy and as a distinct political constituency, began in the mid-1980s and accelerated during the 1990s. This erasure began with the *delegitimization* of women's groups, indeed of virtually all equality-seeking groups as relevant voices in the policy process. This process also eroded the legitimacy accorded to gender units inside of government. Often viewed as a backlash against second-wave feminism, this phase was followed by the *dismantling* of much of the gender-based policy capacity within the federal government and in many of the provinces. Finally, women largely *disappeared* from social policy debates. As suggested earlier, children were identified as the central, if not only legitimate objects of ameliorative social policy, and the women were re-defined, especially in social assistance policy, as genderless individuals with the obligation to be self-sufficient (Brodie 2007).

Delegitimization

The history of the second wave of the Canadian women's movement cannot be recounted here. Suffice it to say that the progressive delegitimization of a "women's voice" in the Canadian policy process began in the mid-1980s and coincided with the ascendancy of neoliberal governing practices, as well as a broader wave of social conservatism that swept over many Western democracies during these years. In Canada, a newly-elected Progressive Conservative government (1984) rather quickly ran into political opposition from the organized women's movement, especially from its flagship, the National Action Committee on the Status of Women (NAC), which strongly objected to the new government's legislative agenda of reducing the state, dismantling universal social programs, empowering the market and, further into its mandate, striking a free trade deal with the United States.

Later in the 1980s, feminism and feminists were regularly disparaged in political debate and in the popular media and, along with other equality-seeking groups, labelled as "special interest" groups. According to this construction, "special interests" stood outside of and in opposition to the interests of "ordinary" Canadians, while federal funding of such groups only served to skew policy priorities and to waste scarce (and undeserved) public resources (Brodie 1995). It was argued that so-called special interest organizations should be funded, not by the public, but by the private constituencies they represented (Dobrowolsky 2004: 187). In other words, equality-seeking groups were considered lobbyists, and should be treated as such.

The rhetoric of special interests, largely imported from the American social conservative movement, veiled a broader backlash against mainstream feminism and its interface with the post-war welfare state. During the past two decades, the most vitriolic case against post-war feminism has been advanced by REAL (realistic, equal, active for life) Women. Labeling itself as "Canada's Alternative Women's Movement," REAL Women's motto is "women's rights but not at the expense of human rights" (www.realwomenca.com). This socially conservative group argued that women's organizations such as NAC did not represent the interests of the vast but silent majority of Canadian women, and could not speak for them in the policy process. As a result of their intensive lobbying, combined with the support of some government backbenchers and members of the Reform Party (a regionally based social conservative party), the Mulroney Conservatives changed the eligibility rules of the WP in the 1980s, allowing for the funding of groups that promoted traditional roles for women as well as patriarchal family values (Dobrowolsky & Jenson 2004, 164–166). Having broken what it saw as a "cozy conspiracy" (Sawer 2006) between feminists inside and outside of the federal government, REAL Women subsequently refrained from seeking federal funds. This refusal was subsequently flagged as a mark of legitimacy, for, according to Gwen Landolt, a long-time REAL Women spokeswoman, "if a group can't support itself and its lobbying activities across the country, then it just isn't a grassroots organization and shouldn't be funded by taxpayers. You have fund-raisers and you earn money, you stand on your two feet, you don't look to government for handouts" (quoted in *Kitchener-Waterloo Record* 2006, A3).

The increasingly unchallenged construction of equality-seeking groups as "special interests" also contributed to the waning influence of gender-based agencies within the federal bureaucracy. From the mid-1980s onward, federal funds designated to improving the status of women were progressively cut back, and previously established gender equality targets began to disappear. Between 1987 and 1990, for example, the Conservative government cut funds to community groups, shelters, and targeted services, while meagre injections of new funding were largely confined to the Canadian Panel on Violence Against Women (1991) as well as related educational and infrastructural initiatives following the 1990 Montreal massacre of 14 women engineering students (Burt and Hardman 2001, 205). Yet, even in the face of this tragedy, the problem of violence against women was progressively re-named and policies re-formulated as one of "family violence," and funding targeted to women's groups doing anti-violence work was cut substantially. There also was a growing backlash against what was dismissively termed as "victim feminism," which allegedly cast all women as an exploited economic underclass or as the prey of batterers and rapists (Brush 2002: 179).

Dismantling

The delegitimization of gender-based citizenship claims on the state was soon followed by the *dismantling* of much of the federal government's gender-based policy capacity, especially after the election of the new Liberal government in 1993. It had its eye firmly set on eliminating the federal deficit and, as discussed above, devolving responsibilities to the provinces, and reducing its long-standing financial commitments in the social policy field. The Canadian Advisory Council on the Status of Women was closed in 1995. Similarly, the federal government's Women's Program, which was charged with providing operational and project funding to women's organizations, was folded into Status of Women Canada (Dobrowolsky 2004: 176–182). In 1995, the Minister

Responsible for the Status of Women was downgraded to the lower status of Secretary of State Responsible for the Status of Women, and thus a designated space for the articulation of women's interests around the federal cabinet table was lost.

This reorganization contradicted a central recommendation of the Beijing Platform for Action that the federal government was preparing to endorse. Paragraph 201 recommends as a best practice that national gender units be located at the highest possible level in federal systems and that these units have access to the forums where the federal division of powers is negotiated (Sawer 2006). In Canada, these locations are unequivocally the executive offices of the prime minister and the premiers, and a seat in the inner cabinet of the governing party. During these same years, Status of Women Canada was progressively downsized and shifted to the margins of the social policy field, most recently being housed under the umbrella of Canadian Heritage. Gendered identity, it would appear, is now coded as just one of many identities that make up the Canadian multicultural mosaic, rather than as a fundamental structuring principle informing the daily lives of Canadians, and a critical component of citizenship equality.

These many changes in the organization of Canada's policy machinery coincided with Canada signing on to the Beijing Platform for Action in 1995, and the federal government's enthusiastic endorsement of gender mainstreaming and gender-based analysis in its Federal Plan for Gender Equality, released the following year. The federal plan committed the government to an encompassing implementation of gender-based analysis in the development of policies, programs, and legislation (SWC 2002: 3). While GBA is discussed in greater detail in Chapter 5 of this report, many academics caution that there are both opportunities and constraints associated with this governing instrument. For example, GBA may not be sufficiently attentive to differences in the needs and priorities of women variously situated by family status, race, sexuality, ethnicity, or class. Neither can GBA effectively engage with the assumptions informing new policy initiatives (Burt and Hardman 2001: 208–211). If, as discussed below, a social problem is framed, however inaccurately, as a problem of children, families, or individuals — rather than being lodged in unequal gender structures — the capacity of GBA to advance women's equality is diminished. Gender-based analysis can also be implemented as an in-house and technocratic exercise that erodes the link between government agencies and the broader community.

The Beijing Platform prescribes that, with respect to all policies and programs, "before decisions are taken, an analysis is made of the effects on women and men."[10] Raising gender to the centre of the full range of public policy is an essential piece in the complicated task of achieving gender equality. As with most policy reforms, however, fewer problems arise with the goals of GBA than with its operationalization and implementation. Policy reform can have unintended and undesirable outcomes. Not the least, as Sawer observed, too often the new language of gender mainstreaming has been used by governments that are less than sympathetic to gender equality to legitimate the dismantling of units with expertise in promoting equal opportunity for women and designated groups (1996). In such cases, gender mainstreaming effectively means that gender-based analysis is both "everywhere and nowhere" in government. In Canada, Status of Women was charged with developing capacities to implement GBA within the federal bureaucracy, but it is not its exclusive responsibility. As Table 8 shows, responsibility for the implementation of GBA is spread across a number of key departments. As important, much of the social policy terrain, which perhaps most requires an intensive GBA analysis, was effectively passed down to the provinces with the elimination of CAP and the creation of the CHST (Burt and Hardman 2001: 213). There is little evidence, moreover, that gender mainstreaming has become an organizing principle in provincial policy-making.

The dismantling of gender-based capacity was also reflected in the reorganization of the federal social bureaucracy in 2003. The division of Human Resources Development Canada (HRDC) into two line departments (Human Resources and Skills Development Canada and Social Development Canada) effectively unraveled the gender-based policy capacities that had been built up within HRDC over the previous decade. Federal bureaucrats once assigned to assessing policy initiatives in terms of gender impacts were redistributed across the two new departments and reassigned to different desks. These desks largely reflected the social policy priorities identified during the lead-up to the signing of the Social Union Framework Agreement (1999) between the federal government and the provinces: children, Canadians with disabilities, and Aboriginal peoples. After the reorganization, SDC maintained its informal gender network while HRSDC did not. With the election of a new Conservative government in 2006 and the recombination of the two departments into Human Resources and Social Development Canada (HRSDC), the fate of these gender-based policy networks in the federal social policy field is uncertain. What is clear is that the repeated reorganization of the social bureaucracy disrupts and disorganizes GBA capacity in this critical policy field.

This dismantling process can also be clearly tracked at the provincial level, especially in Canada's richest provinces, which, as discussed above, adopted the most stringent social assistance regimes and welfare-for-work programs during the 1990s. Alberta was the first to eliminate its gender-based policy machinery when, in 1996, it exercised a sunset clause in its initiating legislation, and eliminated the Alberta Advisory Council on Women's Issues. This arbitrary action met considerable resistance, both from provincial women's groups and opposition parties in the legislature (Harder 2003). The government's response to these objections was characteristic of the kinds of arguments that have been made in Canada and elsewhere by governments determined to dismantle their gender-based policy machinery. One typical response has been that women's organizations have matured and strengthened to the point where they no longer need public support to maintain their capacity to speak to government. As Alberta Minister for Community Development Gary Mar stated at the time:

> Regarding the disposition of the Advisory Council of Women's Issues, I would note that even the federal Liberal government has reached the same conclusion that we have in Alberta; namely that times have changed, women's groups have multiplied and grown in strength, and they can and

want to speak for themselves to government without a publicly funded intermediary (Alberta Assembly Debates, March 27, 1995).

The other typical argument rallied against women's policy agencies was that women are too diverse a constituency to be represented by a single agency. Again, Minister Mar expressed this position during the Alberta legislative debate on the fate of the Alberta Advisory Council:

> [T]he chair of that advisory Council herself has said that women in the province of Alberta speak with many voices; they do not speak with one voice. I happen to agree. As a consequence, it is strongly the view of this government that women cannot be heard and cannot be represented by a single agency. Rather, very clearly women would choose to represent themselves and speak with their own voices (Alberta Assembly Debates, March 25, 1995).

Unlike Alberta, the election of the Harris government in Ontario in 1995 did not see the elimination of the Ontario Women's Directorate, but instead a dramatic downsizing and restructuring of this once large and active gender unit. Established in 1983 and housed in the Office of the Premier, the Women's Directorate immediately saw a reduction in its staff, budget, and influence in the early days of the Harris administration. In 1996, its mandate was changed from the advocacy of women's equality writ large to two policy areas: violence against women, and women and economic development with a special focus on women's entrepreneurship. According to Malloy, the directorate was effectively transformed "into an unmistakable public administration entity with a mandate to 'manage' women's issues, rather than provide an entryway into government for women's movements and their demands" (Malloy 2003: 88, 106).

In British Columbia, one of the first acts of the newly-elected Liberal government in 2001 was to eliminate the province's Ministry of Women's Equality, and over 30 women's centres that had been funded by the provincial government for more than a decade had their funding withdrawn. As Teghtsoonian (2005: 324) explained, "women lost their voice" (2005,

324). The province's gender-based policy capacity has since been confined to Women's Equality and Social Programs, a small sub-unit of the Ministry of Community, Aboriginal and Women's Services. During the same period, the new provincial government also made debilitating cuts to child care, cutting funding to centres and subsidies to low-income parents as well as eliminating training programs for child care workers. The government subsequently assigned responsibility for child care to the Minister Responsible for the Status of Women, thus ensuring that this office would be only partially focused on women's issues. Teghtsoonian (2004: 320) has dubbed this strategy as a gender-diluting function wherein diverse policy responsibilities are subsumed within gender-based units and the gender-specific focus of a portfolio or unit is diffused, if not undermined.

The fate of gender-based units federally, as well as in Alberta, Ontario and British Columbia, appears to support Dobrowolsky's (2004: 188) claim that "there is no doubt then that the neoliberal state diminished political space for women, metaphorically and literally" (2004, 188). The gender units of other provinces, which have not so sharply turned toward neoliberal governing practices, however, share a number of common experiences. First, they report that their budgetary allocations have decreased or remained virtually frozen for the past decade. The 2004 Report of the Women's Advisory Council of Newfoundland and Labrador underlines the implications of a decade and more of fiscal restraint. "The concern from women's equality-seeking organizations," the report notes, "is whether the provincial government will continue with its fiscally driven agenda or listen to the concerns of women and equality-seeking women's organizations" (PACSW 2004). Second, in many provinces, once-autonomous advisory councils now either have been folded into the permanent bureaucracy or communicate with government through actors in the permanent bureaucracy. Finally, many provincial units report the increasing tendency for provincial governments to demand business plans that effectively narrow the range of their research and consultation activities.

Overall, we can conclude that the increased volatility in gender-based policy machinery in Canada during the past decade has had similar consequences to those experienced in countries such as Australia. In assessing the Australian case, Sawer (2006) observed that a continuously changing environment, including the infusion of new public management techniques, has:

- devalued gender-based expertise in favour of management skills;

- deemed it more difficult to evaluate policies at the source for gender impacts and to audit gender outcomes of government activity;

- contributed to an ongoing loss of corporate memory, making it more difficult to sustain the capacities required for the long-term project of advancing gender equality;

- decreased the visibility of gender units, both inside and outside of government; and

- eroded community education functions and severed engagement with community organizations.

Disappearance

The final plank in our review of the capacity of gender units focuses on the disappearance of women as an analytic category in social policy development and, in turn, the erosion of women's equality as a central goal of Canadian public policy. The progressive erasure of gender in governmental discourses, public policy, budgetary priorities, and institutional machinery in the past decade stands in stark contrast to the commitments undertaken by the federal government in signing the Beijing Platform For Action (1995) and elaborated in *Setting the Stage for the Next Century: The Federal Plan for Gender Equality* (SWC 1995). The current invisibility of gender is the outcome of an amalgam of factors that have already been discussed in this report, among them the rise of social con-

servatism and the attendant delegitimization of feminist and all equality-seeking groups as "special interests," the "everywhere and nowhere"
underpinnings of gender mainstreaming, the dismantling of the gender-
based policy machinery, and the erosion of a broader-based women's
movement with strong links to the state.

We focus here on two distinct processes that have reinforced these
tendencies in the social policy field: the elevation of the child (and family) as the priority constitutency of social policy reform, and the laboured
insertion of the genderless individual in contemporary social policy reform thinking. Both developments involved what Lister (2004) called
"the politics of renaming." As Dobrowolsky and Jenson (2004: 172) rightly reminded us, an exploration of the politics of renaming is neither an
academic exercise nor simply a matter of talk. "Representational adjust-
ments to the names of claimants is significant" in understanding how
social policy is framed, which social actors are considered as legitimate
claimants, what kinds of policy interventions are considered appropriate and by whom. However, as we discuss, although contemporary social problems may be framed and analyzed *as if* gender is no longer relevant, the gendered underpinning of these same social problems do not
disappear. To the contrary, they tend to intensify (Bakker and Gill 2003;
Brodie 2003).

As already tracked in Chapter 2, the disappearance of the gendered
subject of social policy can be clearly tracked through federal policy discourses and initiatives of the last decade, which effectively cast the child
as the focal point of social policies. As McKeen (2003: 94–101) documented, the ascendancy of the child as the iconic subject of social policy
reaches back to the late-1980s when the federal government, following
a growing international trend, pledged to end child poverty by the turn
of the millennium. Following the ratification of the UN's Convention on
the Rights of the Child in 1991, the Mulroney government embarked on
what it termed its "child's agenda," concentrating its energies particularly on children at risk. The federal government's almost singular concern with the child and children's poverty intensified during the Chrétien
years, especially after the introduction of the Canadian Child Tax Benefit

and subsequent elaborations such as the National Child Benefit and the Child Disability Benefit.

A textual analysis of Speeches from the Throne across the past two decades graphically demonstrates the progressive disappearance of women as subjects of social policy interventions and the goal of gender equality in official discourses. In the 1980 speech, social policies and programs were discussed in the context of equality for women, and there was explicit discussion of sexual discrimination and violence against women. There also was recognition of the structural impediments to employment facing equality-seeking groups such as native peoples, youth, women, and those with a disability. A similar emphasis on women as a focus of policy targeting is reflected in the Throne speeches throughout the 1980s (1983, 1984, 1986 and 1989). By 1991, however, Throne speeches began to focus on children as "the most vulnerable members of our society," while the family was identified as "the most fundamental building block of Canadian society." By 1994, the social security system and its reform was emphasized and linked to violence against women *and* children. During this period, the problem of violence against women was progressively re-named and policies reformulated as one of family violence. Funding targeted to women's groups doing anti-violence work was cut substantially. A modest reinvestment in the federal government's Family Violence Initiative in the late-1990s, moreover, focused on offenders as well as First Nations (Weldon 2004).

It is important to note that violence against women did not disappear in these years; in fact, the number of women reporting violence and seeking shelter increased. However, federal policy increasingly conveyed the message, both in rhetoric and in practice, that this pervasive social problem was confined to the perpetrators of violence or to particular communities. This politics of re-naming veiled an ongoing social need and shifted resources away from those whose lives had been upset by violence. As Weldon (2004) reported, between 1998 and 2002 the number of women's shelters increased by only 2%, while the number of admissions to existing shelters increased by 20%.

The 1997 post-deficit Throne speech signaled a clear shift in social policy thinking toward the child and families. "Social policy renewal," according to the 1997 speech, identified Canada as "a country that has decided to invest in its children," and whose "objectives as a country" were to "ensure that all Canadian children have the best possible opportunity to develop their full potential." The speech asserted that, "while families have the greatest responsibility in the nurturing and development of our children, they are not alone." This approach to social policy reform was consolidated in the Throne speech of 1999 with the introduction of the National Children's Agenda and the government's objective to reach agreement on "a national action plan to further support parents and families." By 2004, children became the most important social "investment" for the federal government, and the National Child Benefit was singled out (along with Medicare) as Canada's most significant social program. These themes persisted throughout the early 2000s. In the 2002 speech, for example, the government promised "a long-term investment to allow poor families to break out of the welfare trap" and "to increase access to early learning opportunities and to quality child care, particularly for poor and lone-parent families." Across the past decade, progressively from one Throne speech to the next, we witness the virtual erasure of women and gender-based equality claims from official policy discourses.

The goal of eliminating child poverty in Canada was both overdue and necessary, but in many ways the elevation of the abstract "poor child" as the focus of social policy reform incorrectly specified the policy problem. As poverty groups have emphasized time and again, the feminization of poverty is a root cause of child poverty, but the gendered structures of inequality in Canada's labour markets and in society do not enter into a child-centred policy frame (Dobrowolsky and Jenson 2004: 174). Rather, this "politics of naming" effectively set up an opposition between the child and other disadvantaged groups: as a dichotomy between the deserving and undeserving poor as well as between child and parent. Moreover, these policy discourses depict the poor child as a homogeneous category, veiling considerations of how all children are themselves differently configured by, among other things, gender, race, ethnicity, sexuality, and national origin. As Lister (2004: 54) observed, the ascendancy of the homogenized and decontextualized category of child sidesteps structural social divisions that consistently correlate with official definitions and lived experiences of poverty, especially those relating to gender. A child-centred social policy agenda effectively excised women and gender concerns from the official stories of poverty in Canada and, in the process, women's organizations "lost credibility as valuable or legitimate actors in social policy politics" (McKeen 2003: 102).

Beyond the political implications that rebound in the policy process, the children's agenda fails to acknowledge the inescapable fact that, in the vast majority of cases, poor children live with poor women who experience poverty in many different ways. Clearly, gender is a critical factor in the child poverty story. Although women may be erased from the analysis, as Brush (2002: 175) reminded us, most mothers, whether single or not, continue to pay a child penalty (2002, 175). Women's disproportionate share of domestic work and child-caring tasks correlates with labour market discrimination and subsequent inequalities in pay, benefits, and the quality of jobs (Stratigaki 2004: 31). Inadequate provision for social care means many mothers must fashion their labour force participation to accommodate their caring responsibilities. They often are found working part-time in precarious "feminized" sectors of the labour force that offer few cushions if personal circumstances change, such as a relationship breakdown. Many female lone parents who cannot rely on a second wage-earner have little alternative other than to rely on the minimal income provided by provincial and territorial social assistance programs, at least until their children reach school age. In sum, then, the unequal structure of gender and, increasingly, race weaves through both the incidence and the experience of child poverty. The erasure of systemic considerations from social policy analysis, however, does not diminish their persistent effects. In the absence of policies and programs addressing the structural basis of women's poverty, a child care agenda is unlikely to meet its primary objective of reducing child poverty (Paterson et al. 2004: 140).

The disappearance of gender is also related to the increasing promi-
nence of the individual in contemporary social policy reform. As we have
already discussed, many provincial social assistance regimes implicitly
construct welfare recipients as genderless individuals who are expected
to enter the labour force and become self-supporting, regardless of their
personal circumstances or family responsibilities. Exemption from work
requirements afforded to mothers has been systematically reduced in
most provinces. Tax exemptions calculated on the basis of income also
have a strong individualized component. To demonstrate more clearly
the implications of individualization in the social policy field, we draw on
policy documents of the federal government's Policy Research Initiative,
in particular its work on poverty and social exclusion, which were abun-
dant prior to the election of the Harper government in January 2006.

In 1996, the Clerk of the Privy Council established the PRI as a source
of policy advice independent from line departments, which would identify, deepen and integrate the federal government's policy capacity on
highly relevant and emerging crosscutting issues. From its conception,
the PRI has consistently focused on the question of social governance,
exploring such contemporary conceptual innovations as social cohesion, social exclusion, and social capital. In 2003, the PRI launched an
initiative called New Approaches for Addressing Poverty and Exclusion.
This project takes as its point of departure the formative task of reframing "how we think about poverty" and "the levels of inequality we are
willing to tolerate" (Voyer 2004, 1). As discussed below, the PRI invites
us to think about poverty as gender neutral and only marginally affected by broad-based, deeply entrenched, and unequal social structures in
Canadian society.

Individualization, as already noted, is a predominant theme underlying contemporary social policy reform. During the past decade, social
policy regimes in virtually all Western democracies have turned from a
rights-based and redistributive model of social governance toward so-
called "active" welfare policies that place priority on the development
of human capital, individual self-sufficiency, and labour force participation. These reforms are represented as offering the poor a "hand up"

rather than "a hand out." This shift in thinking minimizes, if not explicitly rejects, two critical assumptions that informed the development of the post-war welfare state: social structures systematically advantage some groups and disadvantage others, and public policy appropriately corrects for systemic barriers and inequalities. Individualization masks the ongoing relevance of deeply entrenched inequalities in determining vulnerabilities to poverty as well as capacities to achieve self-sufficiency (Brodie 2008a).

Beck and Beck-Gernsheim (2002: 22–26) characterized individualization as part of a broader contemporary compulsion "to live a life of one's own." As they explained, individualization has a different meaning than individualism, which is generally understood as either self-actualizing or self-seeking behaviour. Individualization, in contrast, places steeply rising demands on people to find personal causes and responses to what are, in effect, collective social problems. In their view, we are all now compelled to find our own "biographic solutions" to systemic contradictions (Beck and Beck-Gernsheim 2002: xxii).

In the process, structural and cyclical unemployment, as well as a broad range of societal barriers, are re-framed in policy thinking as personal shortcomings and behavioural problems (Kitchen 2005: 9). This new governing formula demands that individuals imagine themselves separately from group identities and claims, and conduct their own lives "at pain of economic sanction." Responsibility for social crises that find their genesis in such macro processes as structural unemployment or gendered and racialized labour markets is shifted onto the shoulders of individuals. Living your own life thus includes taking personal responsibility for "your own failures," especially dependency on social assistance. As a result of this "politics of renaming," structurally disadvantaged groups such as women or racial minorities are "collectively individualized" both in popular cultural representations and in public policy (Beck and Beck-Gernsheim 2002: 23–27). In other words, members of disadvantaged groups are invited to deny or discount the social forces that have situated them differently and unequally from other Canadians.

Individualization re-defines poverty as arising from personal deficits with respect to, among other things, skills development, moral direction, social capital and self-discipline. Contemporary social policy reform thus aspires to correct the apparent deficiencies of poor people through discipline, coercion, skills enhancement, and various technologies of self-help. The PRI's 2003 research theme on poverty and social exclusion thus stands out as a concerted and often laboured attempt to refract the experience of poverty in Canada through the lens of individualization. Using cohort data gathered from Canadians during the past decade as empirical grounding, the PRI understands poverty as something that happens over an individual's life course — the result of missed opportunities, bad decisions, or unfortunate events — rather than as a reflection of either structural inequalities or of life-cycle effects. According to this analysis, poverty, for the vast majority, is a "fluid and temporary" experience: entry and exit from low income is associated with events and transitions that occur over the course of one's life, such as changes in family or employment status (Kunz and Frank 2004: 4–5). The PRI next asserts that individuals normally have (or should have) the resources to ride out these temporary experiences of "being poor." "Individuals," PRI researchers contend, "usually have a set of resources at their disposal, including personal characteristics, social relations, human and financial resources, and government support. If these buffers are not strong enough to overcome life's calamities...individuals risk being at the margins of society" (Kunz and Frank 2004: 5).

Having untied the experience as well as governmental responses to poverty from their structural moorings, the PRI does concede that there are identifiable sub-groups in the general population — about 8% of working age Canadians in 1996 — for whom poverty is neither temporary nor fluid. Canada's "persistently poor" are largely confined to five groups: lone-parent families, unattached older individuals, persons with work-limiting disabilities, Aboriginal peoples living off reserves, and recent immigrants (arriving in Canada in the 1990s). These at-risk groups are five to nine times more likely to experience long-term poverty than other Canadians (Hatfield 2004: 19, 22). While conceptually distinct, these groups, according to the PRI, "share a number of things in common. Each group carries an identity marker defined by an event occurring over the course of life, ranging from a change in family status or lack thereof, a change in health status, or a change in place of residence." "Departure from some of these characteristics," the researchers add, "reduces the risks of long-term poverty" (Kunz and Frank 2004: 5).

The PRI offers the following advice for "avoiding persistent low income for members of all high-risk groups" (Hatfield 2004: 22). The most important factor identified is attachment to paid work followed by the following individualized strategies:

- exit from a high-risk group;

- draw on spouse for support;

- belong to only one high-risk group;

- graduate from high school; or

- live in a region with a high employment rate (Hatfield 2004: 22–23).

The PRI's conceptual breakthrough is a quintessential example of neoliberal individualization. Although it identifies Canada's poor by group-based markers, its proposed strategies for poverty alleviation are framed in terms of individual choices and private solutions. In effect, Canada's persistently poor are advised to get a job, get married, and move to Alberta. As such, this policy advice simultaneously downloads all responsibility for structural inequalities and risk management onto individuals (Brush 2002: 168) and validates the market as the primary mechanism whereby individuals secure personal security and well-being (Clarke 2004: 90–91). This formulation, of course, does not recognize the many contributions to human well-being that are generated outside the market, through unpaid care, kinship, social citizenship, solidarity, and political equality.

Table 9 shows the poverty rates for the groups the PRI identified as experiencing persistent low income between 1996 and 2001, and the 2001 Census data of poverty rates for women in these groups. These data are

TABLE 9 *Poverty Rates among Marginalized Groups*

	% of Group in Persistent Low Income 1996–01	% of Women in Poverty in 2001 (before tax)
Lone parents	22	38*
Individuals with a disability	26	26
Recent immigrants	26	35
Aboriginal people off reserve	16	36
Unattached	26	41**

* After tax. ** LICO.
Sources For 1996–01 Hatfield (2004: 3); for women in 2001 Townson (2005: 2–3), NCW (2001).

drawn from different sources and are not intended to provide a systematic comparison. They do, however, betray three glaring flaws in the individualizing politics of renaming. The first striking observation to be drawn from these data is that these are largely structural identity markers from which the poor cannot realistically depart. Indeed, among the five groups only two — lone parents and unattached individuals — would appear to be able to depart from their marker, most obviously through marriage. In contrast, persons with work-limiting disabilities generally cannot simply choose to transcend the physical, social, and institutional constraints associated with disability. Neither can Aboriginal peoples, on or off reserves, depart easily from a historical legacy of social and institutional racism.

Related to this, the term "recent immigrant" masks the fact that the vast majority of recent immigrants in Canada are people of colour and thus race rather than length of residency may be the critical marker underlying the growing incidence of poverty among this group. This suspicion is supported by a recent study conducted for the Canadian Labour Congress, which reported that racial discrimination is a large contributing factor to poor labour market outcomes for Canada's racialized workers. It found that Canadian-born men of colour and immigrant women of colour have the highest unemployment rates in Canada. The finding that Canadian-born workers of colour are doing badly cannot be explained away by reference to lack of Canadian credentials and expertise (Cheung 2005).

Second, and as important for our purposes, individualization purports to transcend "old" political debates about systemic inequalities, but the traces of gender cannot be erased, either empirically or conceptually, from this script of social policy reform. Available gender-disaggregated poverty statistics demonstrate that most of the PRI's five categories of the persistently poor are internally skewed by gender. Finally, these data demonstrate that individualization discourses veil the different incidence of poverty among women. The gender-aggregated data veil the unacceptably high rates of poverty among these marginalized women.

These data on crosscutting gender disparities are neither new nor surprising. Among other things, they reflect many of the factors already discussed in this report: a deeply entrenched gendered division of labour that assigns to women the weight of unpaid social reproductive work, low pay in feminized job ghettos, precarious part-time work that affords few benefits or other forms of income security in later life, and few governmental supports for either child and elder care or training programs and skills upgrading. Renaming women as well as members of other socially disadvantaged groups as individuals does not erase the spaces they occupy in the economy or the household. We do indeed live our own lives and we are the authors of our own biographies, but we do so within entrenched and often inequitable social contexts (Brodie 2008a).

This said, the PRI's advice to the persistently poor to get a job or depend on a spouse must be read with considerable skepticism. Although the market is represented as the most important source of human welfare, it is not a neutral mechanism. Markets have proved themselves, time and again, to be notorious places of discrimination, exploitation, harassment, stress, and exclusion. It is thus far from axiomatic that paid work is a passport to social inclusion, especially in an increasingly polarized labour market. Bad jobs may only provide what Sen has identified as "unfavourable inclusion or disempowering inclusion."[11] Individualization invites women to embrace the stereotypical "male biography" (Esping-Anderson 1999: 70) of worker–breadwinner, but few women are able to draw on the reservoir of unpaid domestic and caring work on which this role has traditionally depended. The PRI allows that the persistently poor also can escape low income by depending on a spouse and presumably taking up this unpaid work. Neither model, however, speaks to the lived realities of most working women who struggle on a daily basis to balance the simultaneous demands of paid work and unpaid caring responsibilities, or the multiple and intersecting axes of social vulnerability.

An individualized formulation stands in stark contrast to feminist analyses of inclusion/ exclusion which emphasize the "absence, marginalization, and exclusion of women in different situations, but women's position with respect to power relations in the public, private, and symbolic domains" (Daly and Saraceno 2002: 84). Moreover, feminists stress the interdependence of power relations across these domains. While contemporary social policy reform advocates rehabilitating those at the margins, the source of marginalization often rests at the centre, especially in the prevailing gender order that mediates the interface between production and social reproduction (Daly and Saraceno 2002: 100).

Five

Budgets and Social Policy

THE DISAPPEARANCE OF gender in social policy thinking complements the ascendancy of budgets in the formulation and prioritization of public policies in the last decade. An increasingly important component of social policy capacity is the entire process of budget planning. The past two decades have been marked by the fiscalization of social policies and the prioritization of fiscal health over the well-being of Canadians in need. In the past decade, policy decisions were steered through a period of dramatic cuts between 1994–95 and 1996–97, followed by a surplus era (1998–) where previous cuts were not significantly redressed. Indeed, in the surplus era the federal government focused on two policy instruments to influence social policy: tax credits/refunds and federal-provincial/territorial agreements that involved earmarked unconditional increases to the CHST. Between 1998 and 2004, $152 billion was allocated to tax cuts (which mainly benefited higher income earners and large corporations), $61 billion was allocated to paying down the debt, and $34 billion were net new resources to provinces for health and child care. In addition, changes to EI, which directly resulted in fewer women qualifying to receive benefits and reduced benefit rates, were not reversed. As Yalnizyan (2005a: 7) noted:

Remarkably little of the increase in new funds actually spent in this seven-year period was devoted specifically to enhancing the security of Canada's most vulnerable individuals — through the building of affordable housing, the provision of quality child care, the reduction of the costs of post-secondary education and training, the expansion of immigrant settlement services, or the assurance of benefit coverage of part-time and causal workers, including adequate benefits for the unemployed. Taken together, the federal government's new spending initiatives in these areas would not have been more than $5 billion over the seven-year period.

The single most significant initiative targeted at poverty reduction — the Canada Child Tax Benefit — amounted to only 10% of the total costs of the federal tax reform agenda. Additional tax credits — for caregivers and child care — were of no help to women with no taxable income.

In sum, three sets of issues link social policy to the budget process.

1. The federal government continues to act unilaterally in the social policy field through secrecy of the budget process and a hierarchy of interest representation in the pre-consultation process.

2. Social policy has not been open to public consultations, nor have indicators, social audits, or shared best practices been developed in a systematic way that would concretize the principles of the Social Union Framework Agreement.

3. Social questions remain secondary to the priorities of financial markets and sound economic policies, hiding the reality that all macroeconomic policies are implicitly social policies with distributional consequences along regional, gender, race, and class lines (Elson and Cagatay 2000).

With this context in mind, we assess the following:

• How are fiscal priorities determined?

- What are the current mechanisms and capacities for aligning policy commitments with allocated resources (policy coherence)?

- What gender-based monitoring capacities are in place to "follow the money?"

- What types of accountability are embedded in the budget process, and who participates?

The Determination of Fiscal Policies

Several aspects of how fiscal policies are determined can be considered. The first set of issues relates to the process itself, pre-budget consultations and their effectiveness in terms of a broad representation of societal interests. The second set of questions involves the broader issue of how fiscal/macro policies are defined, and the role of social policy and women's unpaid labour within those current definitions.

Decision making about fiscal policy and, by extension, social policy is largely concentrated in the hands of finance ministries and central banks that are said to have the requisite expertise and reflect the rebalancing of power among ministries and agencies within government. The worldwide trend toward independent central banks has been reinforced by the widespread implementation of fiscal restraint legislation as well as balanced budget laws.[12]

In the case of Canada, three key architects dominate the overall budget process: the Privy Council Office, the Department of Finance, and the Treasury Board. The Privy Council Office ensures that individual ministers and government departments consider the budgetary priorities of the prime minister when making policy and financial decisions. The Treasury Board is actually a committee of Cabinet and consists of six ministers responsible for the management of expenditure through targets and human resources in the public service. Finance is responsible for policy decisions (e.g., tax rates and structures) and the minister establishes the fiscal framework for all government departments and agencies. Effectively, the federal budget is written by civil servants within the

Department of Finance, with political direction steered by the minister of finance and the prime minister. The governor of the Bank of Canada also meets weekly with the finance minister to consult on monetary policy (Makarenko 2005). Nevertheless, it is the Bank's mandate to use monetary action in mitigating fluctuations in the general level of production, trade prices and employment (Parkinson 2002). In other words, the Bank has historically performed all three functions, but at present price stability is the Bank's primary monetary policy. While price stability is a desirable goal, it should not necessarily be the only macroeconomic goal of central banks. However, due to unequal representation in the policy formulation and institutional processes of economic governance, more political weight is given to "technocrats," that is, neo-classical economists, financial administrators and central bankers, who may not be representative of broader societal interests. They are often trained within the mainstream orthodoxies that emphasize price stability at the expense of employment creation, as well as a smaller, market-supporting role for government and greater freedom of markets.

The federal-level budget process has become somewhat more open to consultation and public input. However, this has mainly taken the form of consultations on draft legislation with tax professionals, such as lawyers and accountants, and a more open and formal pre-budget consultation process through the House of Commons Standing Committee on Finance. As Philipps (2005: 12–13) noted, "there is no doubt these consultations make a valuable contribution to the tax policy process." But she goes on to note: "Tax professionals cannot be expected to represent all of the public interest despite their superior understanding of how the rules work. This raises the challenging question of how other sections of the public can be given an effective voice in fiscal policy-making." Currently, there appears to be a clear hierarchy of interests represented before the Finance Committee, with equality-seeking groups and social activists often appearing together and separate from those representing industry interests. This necessarily puts real constraints on social policy debates and planning. Even elected representatives have little substantial influence over the budget because of the sanctions of our Westminster style of parliamentary government, the convention of party discipline, and the budget's status as a matter of confidence (Philipps 2006).

Philipps (2005: 14) suggests that improvements in the pre-budget consultation process might include:

- more actively seeking out participation of diverse organizations and experts;

- funding pre-consultation sessions through resources for those groups often hard pressed in terms of time and money;

- enhanced use of the electronic resources to explain the budget process;

- a final Committee report that expresses the full range of views represented; and

- conducting more focused hearings on one or two issues that would veer away from the similar general presentations made each year.

The foregoing analysis suggests that studying the politics of the budget process is essential to understanding how the distribution of power within that process affects the subsequent distribution of public resources around social policy. The concept of power can be understood in the traditional sense of power as formal structures, but more recent perspectives also see power as the informal incorporation of dominant norms and values into information systems, legitimizing certain knowledge forms and realizing these through bureaucratic practices and procedures. Unequal power relations within the budget process can be expressed by:

- inclusion or exclusion of different social groups to the decision-making process; and

- norms and values explicitly expressed and embedded in the priorities, assumptions and content of the budget (Norton and Elson 2002: 23).

A second set of concerns about *how* macroeconomic parameters are drawn and how social policies fit into that frame has been raised by heterodox economists. As Elson and Cagatay (2000: 1357) suggested, if the advice given to the Department of Finance and the governor of the Bank of Canada prioritizes maintaining short-run "credibility" with financial institutions, and if maintaining debt service payments takes precedence over all other interests, then the entitlements of those who own financial assets are systematically prioritized ahead of those who only own their labour. From women's perspectives, this hierarchy of interest representation is particularly harmful, as women possess fewer financial assets than men and rely on social policy to meet the gaps between paid labour, care work and social provisioning. However, with even further tax reductions, the economic capacity to draw on in order to finance collective needs for maintaining and expanding social infrastructure is being undermined through this planned decline in the share of taxation in the economy (Yalnizyan 2005b:17).

Feminist and heterodox economists have been critical of the conventional macroeconomic framework that guides fiscal, monetary, and exchange rate policy. Researchers have argued that gender-neutral macroeconomic policy will only address women's needs and experiences to the extent to which they conform to male norms. But a substantial part of women's time and resources is dedicated to unpaid work — the work of producing and caring for human beings — which underpins the paid economy. This omission of the activities and values left out of macroeconomic inquiry and therefore policy is not simply an omission based on complexities of measurement. Rather, it reflects assumptions built into this model that exclude women's time in unpaid work as a used economic resource. In the last decade, feminist researchers have documented how neoliberal economic policies cut social supports and rely on women's unpaid labour to fill the gaps. In this sense, current fiscal policies treat women's unpaid work as an externality. As Lahey (2005) reported, women's ongoing responsibilities for unpaid work push them in the direction of part-time and other marginal forms of work, which generate smaller incomes and benefits, making them more dependent on the very redistributive social policies that have been dramatically scaled back. Policy makers are rarely explicit about how such assumptions guide their decision making. Yet social policy development in Canada is informed by these implicit (and often paradoxical) models of the macro economy (Bakker 1997), the family, and models of social policy.

As we noted, in the last decade Canadian policy-makers have relied on a simultaneous strategy of *familialization* and *individualization* when it comes to social policy. Both aspects of such a strategy *degender* individuals and reinforce a market-based model of provisioning. Indeed, many of the trends in budgetary practice reflect a shift toward this market-based citizenship with norms of increased self-reliance and private responsibility. This discourse erases gender and substitutes citizens for taxpayers. Moreover, because gender identity has been rapidly displaced as an organizing thread in social policy, it is increasingly difficult for women, as a group, to make collective claims on the state for equality, resources, or security (Brodie 1995).

Mechanisms for Social Policy Coherence Inside and Outside of Governments

In Canada, there is no systematic annual process within government to evaluate budgets from a gender-sensitive perspective. In fact, as noted above, the capacity of provincial and federal governments to undertake gender-based analysis of spending and taxation measures is very low, as fewer and fewer direct resources are allocated to gender expertise within governments. This is despite the fact that the budget is increasingly a key vehicle for delivering social policy objectives, including commitments to gender equality.

Status of Women Canada has undertaken a number of specific gender-sensitive analyses of the federal budget. In 2004, for instance, SWC prepared a report on that year's budget that contrasted various budget statements related to key policy areas, such as health care, with specific comments by the Minister Responsible for the Status of Women that highlight some of the general gender-based impacts. In 2002, a study on gender mainstreaming reviewed the policy environments and the capacity to undertake gender-based analysis, as well as cases where effective interventions had taken place (Health Canada, Department of Justice). These are important contributions to foregrounding gender-based analysis in the budget and program planning process, yet they are limited by the fact that they:

- are one-time exercises rather than annual oversight mechanisms;

- bypass the Department of Finance as a key co-ordinator of fiscal policy; and

- place the burden on SWC to provide the expertise for the development of tools and indicators. For a sustainable process to be realized, this means facilitating an internal process within each department that reflects its culture and norms rather than relying on an outside body to conduct a gender-based analysis (Teghtsoonian 2004; Hoskyns 2004).

In 2005, the Parliamentary Standing Committee on the Status of Women (FEWO) released a report on gender-based analysis within the federal government (FEWO 2005a). The Committee expressed its disappointment with the lack of effective implementation of gender-based analysis in Canada despite the advanced tools and training modules that have been developed within government. The Committee also found an uneven process of gender-based analysis across departments and programs. In terms of the Department of Finance and the budget process, the Committee found that there was no regular *systematic* effort to incorporate gender-based analysis into the budget process. It called for the Department to take a leadership role in this process. "Canada does not have an effective process to do a gender analysis of the budget. It would expect that the Department of Finance could assign a senior official the responsibility for implementing a gender-analysis process which would allow the department to take a leadership role internationally in gender-budgeting" (FEWO 2005a: 33).

In the government response to the report (FEWO 2005b), it made a commitment to appoint a gender-based analysis champion within the Department of Finance who would, in conjunction with SWC, create a pilot project to train a group of analysts and managers on the application of gender-based analysis. The government made similar commitments within Treasury Board and the Privy Council. We make recommendations in the conclusion of this study on how to begin to mobilize such a process in the short term.

Practical governmental initiatives *do* exist elsewhere, in the European Union and throughout the Commonwealth (Commonwealth Secretariat 2002). For instance, in the United Kingdom the Women's Budget Group, an independent organization bringing together academics and people from non-governmental organizations and trade unions, works with Her Majesty's Treasury to encourage a gender budget for the United Kingdom by advising and consulting with Treasury officials and meeting with Treasury ministers. In the spring of 2003, in conjunction with the Women and Equality Unit, the Women's Budget Group launched the pilot Gender Analysis of Expenditure Project (GAP) across several departments. Members and staff of the Budget Group worked closely with Treasury officials, providing technical advice and assisting with project management. The Final Report of the Gender Analysis of Expenditure Project was published in July 2004 (UK 2004).

Another innovative example of gender-based analysis and budget processes is drawn from the international level of the United Nations. In a major study on gender mainstreaming within the United Nations Budget and Planning process, sponsored by the Inter-agency Task Force on Gender Mainstreaming, researchers focused on the extent to which gender-based analysis is incorporated into budget narratives, manuals, instructions, and the key components of results-based budgeting: objectives, accomplishments, indicators and outputs. The focus was on the planning cycle, from issuance of budget instructions, through the process of drafting the program budget text, to the program budget content, to monitoring and assessment functions.

A technical expert in the Women's Budget Group outlined a series of exercises on how government departments, starting with Finance (Treasury), might conduct a gender-based analysis of the budget process. The complexity and the demands they place on analysts vary.

1. The simplest level of analysis is a counting exercise that makes gender visible by highlighting the number of women and men affected by a particular policy. A requirement is to have nationally representative data that are sex disaggregated.

2. The next level involves an audit of the incidence of revenues and/or expenditure. This is similar to what Yalnizyan and Phillips have done in their work in Canada. The goal is to reveal bias in the design of policies that result in revenue being collected from or expenditures on that are disproportionate to women or men. As the Canadian case illustrates, disaggregated expenditure statistics are rarely presented in government accounts and measuring tax incidence across women and men is complicated by questions of fiscalization and the use of indirect taxation and the levelling of taxation at the household rather than individual level. The further question of spending according to needs versus parity of spending on the sexes must also be considered here.

3. Gender impact assessment is therefore the next level of analysis which moves beyond making gender visible or accounting for the incidence of government expenditure. Here the focus is on the short- and long-run effects of the budget on gender differentials in the distribution of resources, work, gender norms and roles. Time-use surveys and satellite accounts of unpaid work become part of the data required. Canada has the capacity to undertake this form of analysis given Statistics Canada's excellent long-term work on collecting data on unpaid activities. Using micro-level data, a model of income distribution will also capture the distributional impacts of the budget on individual and family resources in the short

term. More long-term gender differentiated changes in behaviour can be measured by linking to other behaviours, such as labour market participation, changes in gender segregation and "appropriate" roles for women and men.

4. Gender mainstreaming is the broadest type of analysis as it relates to the introduction of a gender-based analysis across the entire policy and planning process. Method 2 of gender-based analysis within the United Nations systems, discussed below, is an example of this approach. Mainstreaming applies to all departments and involves a good deal of co-ordination.

5. Benchmarking, a popular tool within the European Union (applied especially to poverty) establishes a minimum standard and a time frame over which it is to be met. For benchmarking to be effective, it needs to be clearly tied to policies, which will be effective in realizing those benchmarks. While this sounds simple, in practice it requires a series of social choices and deeper understanding about the links between macroeconomic policy and the structures of gender inequalities (Rake 2002).

The table in Appendix A summarizes these methods of analyses, raises questions explored under each and documents the resource requirements for undertaking such a level of analysis in the budget process.

The methodology used relied on a content analysis of budget and planning documents, a series of extensive interviews with different actors in that process, and a number of concrete drafting exercises targeted at specific actors in the budget and planning process. These included senior managers, members of the budget/planning branch, gender focal points, program staff and oversight/evaluation staff. Recommendations for each entity were made based on the site visits and evaluations of the two experts. The importance of assessing change over time was also institutionalized through a series of outcome-based indicators (Beck and Bakker 2002). A key result of the UN study was to facilitate a dialogue within departments among officials who did not necessarily communicate with each other on a regular basis and to make explicit the ways in which gender-based analysis was relevant to their everyday work. This then became part of the process. Another important finding was that no generic instructions or manual could be developed, given the different cultures and approaches to budgeting within entities. Finally, the exercise had the biggest impact in entities where little connection appeared to exist in the eyes of the planners between gender mainstreaming and their program of work.

We offer a series of recommendations to encourage a similar process within the federal government, starting with the Department of Finance. These recommendations build on the government response to the second report of the Standing Committee on the Status of Women, entitled *Gender-Based Analysis: Building Blocks for Success,* and are meant to enhance both social policy coherence and gender impact assessment.

A number of *outside government* initiatives aim to "follow the money" from the vantage point of women, the poor, and lower-income groups. The mounting interest in independent and applied budget work recognizes the importance of budgets as both technical and political documents. Applied budget analysis offers a new tool for ensuring government accountability to international and national commitments, as well as a balanced distribution of public resources.

The Canadian Feminist Alliance for International Action (FAFIA) has taken the most ambitious initiative in this area. They commissioned Armine Yalnizyan (2005a), a leading progressive feminist economist, to undertake a gender budget analysis (the first of its kind in Canada) of federal budgets from 1995 to 2004. Yalnizyan (2005b) also prepared an assessment of the 2005 federal budget, the findings of which we have referred to earlier in this report. These documents provide a compelling argument for a systemic gender-based analysis of the entire federal budget to be conducted within the Department of Finance. Without such an effort, Yalnizyan concluded, we will continue with a lack of policy coherence between national and international commitments to gender equality and the monies dedicated to those goals, especially social policy objectives.

The CCPA's Alternative Federal Budget, a collaborative project of civil society organizations, is another example of linking participatory budgets to overall macroeconomic planning. The Alternative Budget group produces a comprehensive parallel budget to that of the government, linking it to a medium-term macroeconomic framework (CCPA nd). In 2006, the Alternative Federal Budget collaboration launched a concerted effort to undertake a gender budget analysis, and several technical papers are available on the CCPA website that link gender to spending and taxation policies (see also AFB 2008 for a gender based analysis).

Notwithstanding the momentum of some of these efforts, much needs to be done by governments, multilateral institutions, and other actors to indicate their commitment to budgetary processes that will be viewed as credible to the full range of stakeholders in society. Rhetorical commitments of greater sensitivity to the interests of the poor, vulnerable groups, and to gender equity need to be reinforced with binding commitments, for example, commitments that have the force of law. This requires governments to live up to their stated commitments and to re-think and reallocate their budgetary priorities in dialogue with a wider range of stakeholders. Above all, it requires the sustained political commitment by senior officials and program directors.

In sum, a gender mainstreaming approach to the budget planning and policy process is increasingly important due to the reliance on budgets as instruments for administering various aspects of social policy (fiscalization). Second, it also reflects a broader emerging consensus that social policy needs to be mainstreamed into macroeconomic analysis, as all macroeconomic policies entail a variety of social outcomes that need to be made explicit (Elson and Cagatay 2000: 1348). Third, a common theme in entitlement and rights-based approaches to the provision of public services is "the importance of translating international human rights norms into national budget processes through establishing entitlements to resources and standards of service delivery" (Norton and Elson 2002: viii). We explore these aspects of gender and budgets by highlighting how various notions of accountability reflect the prevailing balance of interests and pressures in the public expenditure management system. As the last decade reveals, federal budgets have consistently prioritized debt reduction over social policy spending. While the current system does not reflect a gender-equitable, nor indeed pro-poor orientation, we suggest there are a number of avenues for incrementally building on positive elements of the existing framework, provided the political will is there.

Accountability of What to Whom?

Canada has been a signatory to a number of UN commitments to gender equality and more inclusive economic development over the last few decades, such as the Convention on the Elimination of All Forms of Discrimination against Women (CEDAW), the Beijing Platform of Action, and, more recently, the Millennium Development Goals. The 1990s saw the emergence of an international consensus on poverty eradication and the promotion of gender equality through such policy commitments as the 1995 World Social Summit on Development, The Fourth World Conference on Women in Beijing, and the International Conference on Population and Development. Signatory countries made commitments to integrate the goals of these conferences into their policy plans (SWC 1995). This included mobilizing resources and ensuring transparency and accountability in budget processes, as well as monitoring progress toward these goals precisely because of the documented links between gender equality and broader economic and social progress.

However, a number of significant shortfalls and inconsistencies in meeting these targets were identified in the 10-year reviews in 2005 of the UN Fourth World Conference on Women. A key obstacle has been the inadequate allocation of, and ineffective and inequitable use of public resources. In January 2003, the UN Committee on the Elimination of Discrimination against Women identified underfunding of key social supports on which women heavily rely as an impediment to Canada's fulfillment of key human rights commitments to women. One problem in implementing the Platform for Action and Canada's obligations under various UN treaties is that there is often a disconnection between policy development, budget appropriations, and the outcomes of policies. The processes are different and governments often have difficulties bringing them together. A gender-sensitive budget analysis can bring the processes together by comparing international commitments to human rights, social entitlements, and gender equality with resources and services. Indeed, then Minister of Finance Ralph Goodale made a public commitment to undertake gender budget analysis in Canada in the 2006 budget (Hansard, February 7, 2005). No such initiative is under way, despite the fact that Canadian international funding agencies are expected to undertake gender impact assessments of all projects carried out in developing countries.

This neglect of gender-based analysis in budgets raises a broader question for policy makers: to whom is fiscal policy in Canada accountable? Conventionally, the answer has been taxpayers. Generically defined but *de facto*, fiscal policy is accountable to all citizens who are current, former, and future taxpayers (for example, seniors and children). However, as feminist economists, lawyers, and activists have pointed out, taxpayers are not generic subjects, but men and women with different socioeconomic realities. Furthermore, there is widespread recognition that these are not monolithic groups; they are marked by social conditions such as class, race, sexual orientation, age and disability. Hence, the issue of equality among various groups in society becomes an important component for analyzing budgets and the delivery of social policy. Second, fiscal policy is connected to an overall macroeconomic framework within which other economic activities are seen to take place. This involves a primary orientation to markets (financial, labour, etc.) versus people.

Specifically, government accountability in the budget and planning process tends to prioritize market participants in two senses: through a general and indirect form of *market accountability* related to sustaining an "appropriate business climate" of concern to investors, businesses, currency traders, etc.; and a second form of more direct and specific *accountability of borrowers to lenders (creditors)* — in short, to all of the institutions that might fund budget deficits through loans. A third form of *social accountability* involving desired social outcomes, such as equity, distributive justice, provisioning of needs for all, and social inclusion, is a conditional form of accountability in current institutional planning, as it is secondary to the "soundness" of macroeconomic policies. We begin with a critical consideration of the accountability of institutions within the federal context before turning to the budget process and its capacity to mainstream gender to ensure more inclusive and effective social policies.

Within this context, budgetary policies must be comprehensively defined so all aspects of government expenditures and income (including taxation) are placed on the table for consideration by the various stakeholders — including equality-seeking groups. This presupposes an institutional and political framework that is responsive to popular needs, as well as transparency, so decisions can be debated on the basis of timely, useful, and accurate information.

Within the conventional frame of macroeconomic analysis used in Canada and elsewhere, social policy is secondary to "sound" macroeconomic policies, and conditions of market accountability trump conditions of social citizenship. Elson and Cagatay (2000: 1347–1348) argued that an alternative approach to seeing social policies as an afterthought to macroeconomic policies "would start with the premise that all macroeconomic policies are enacted within a certain set of distributive relations and institutional structures; and that all macroeconomic policies entail a variety of social outcomes that need to be made explicit." This type of outlook would mean that sound economic policies are judged not only by market-based criteria (and those that signal the appropriate business climate), but in terms of desired social outcomes, such as distributive justice, equity, and provisioning of needs for all (Elson and Cagatay 2000: 1348).

This new approach raises the relationship between accountability and macroeconomic policy. Given these two layers of accountability: Who is involved in decisions about aggregate levels of spending, taxation and public debt? What are the economic views of those who currently make these decisions? A discussion of accountability needs to consider each of these dimensions and the degree to which they enable or constrain the formulation of budgets and social policy that are gender sensitive and reflect the social principles stated above. Part of a revised budgetary practice would clarify the parameters and variables included in decisions, as well as highlighting who sets the bounds and who does the adjusting in relation to changes in social policy. By seeking out the social content in macroeconomic policies, we begin to see how macroeconomic policy processes and budgetary practices can be transformed in a more inclusive and negotiated way (Elson and Cagatay 2000: 1360).

To sum up, the combination of reduced capacity inside government to undertake gender-based analysis, especially in areas of macroeconomic policy, in conjunction with the drastic reduction in, or abandonment of social entitlements for health care, welfare services, and employment insurance, illustrate the *3Ds* we mentioned at the outset of this study: the *delegitimization* of women's voices in the policy process, the *dismantling* of gender-based agencies, and the *disappearance* of the gender subject as a necessary component of social policy thinking and reform.

Six

Recommendations

Opening Up a National Debate about the Conditions to Be Attached to the CST

Recommendation: That relevant line departments within the federal government and the provinces, in partnership with relevant gender units and non-governmental research and advocacy organizations, facilitate a national debate about both the national objectives to be pursued through the Canada Social Transfer as well as the creation of social policies that would better enable Canadians to achieve a sustainable work–life balance.

As this report has demonstrated, after the elimination of CAP and the introduction of an unconditional block fund, the CHST, Canada's social assistance regime has eroded and fragmented into 13 separate provincial-territorial systems. While some of these systems have imposed more stringent conditions on the receipt of social welfare than others, all are inadequate and all contribute to the ongoing feminization of poverty in Canada, as well as unacceptably high levels of child poverty. In 2004, two separate block funds were introduced: the Canada Health Transfer, which is governed by the conditions of the *Canada Health Act,* and the Canada Social Transfer. The CST fund involves the transfer of approximately $15 billion in cash and tax points from the federal government to the provinces, to be used for social programs and for post-secondary education. But there are no conditions attached to how this money should be divided between these two provincial responsibilities, or mechanisms to ensure transparency or accountability.

Canadians have not been invited into a national debate about the levels and kinds of support that should be provided to Canada's most vulnerable citizens. Although civil society organizations have invited Canadians and their governments to engage in this debate, such calls have yet to gain any momentum (CCSD 2004). Indeed, most Canadians are not well informed about the minimum levels of support afforded to Canada's poor, the patchwork of conditions and constraints across the provinces that make it more or less difficult for social assistance recipients to provide for their families, or the gendered, racial and ability biases that these programs both aggravate and perpetuate. Increasing evidence of the racialization of poverty, as well as entrenched rates of poverty among Canada's Aboriginal peoples and female-headed, sole-parent families stand in stark opposition to the values Canadians consistently endorse and entrust their governments to protect and promote. Canadians should take their governments up on their commitments in the SUFA to "ensure opportunities for Canadians to have meaningful input into social policies and programs."

For almost a decade, governments in Europe have been engaged in research and policy formation designed to address the constraints the majority of families now confront in negotiating a sustainable work–life balance. Gender has been placed at the centre of this new thinking. Indeed, a noted welfare state theorist, who wrote a widely cited report on social policy reform for the European Union in 2000, has argued that gender equity is the "lynchpin of any positive post-industrial equilibrium between households and the economy" (Esping-Anderson 2002: 69). Governments must put gender back into the social policy equation, he argued, because contemporary economic and political realities require both women's productive and social reproductive labour. However, rather than embrace the challenge of establishing equitable work–life balance social policies, as this report explains, Canadian governments, for the most part, have engaged in the politics of renaming by prioritizing child-centred social policy and individualization strategies. As this report also demonstrates, neither strategy can veil the inescapable conclusion that social policy is also gender policy and that, as Lister (2004: 55) reminded us, "the conceptual and methodological implications go well beyond adding women in."

Canadian governments (except Quebec) in the SUFA committed both to respect the equality, rights and dignity of all Canadian women and their diverse needs, as well as provide appropriate assistance to those in need. Status of Women Canada should take the lead in specifying how these commitments could and should take form within the context of transformative changes in family form, dual earner families, and increasingly diversified communities.

Tracking Gender Outcomes in the Federal System

Recommendation: That the federal government and the provinces should create new mechanisms for intergovernmental co-ordination of policy goals, transparency and accountability, and best practices, such as the open method of co-ordination developed by the European Union for these purposes. Status of Women Canada should, in conjunction with relevant departments, explore the experience of this method with respect to co-ordinating gender-focused social policies.

As noted in this report, Canada's social policy regime has been residualized and fragmented during the last decade. The Canadian federation now faces a situation where each province has different views on how to address social needs or define social progress. This is partly due to the absence of conditions attached to the CHST and the CST, as well as to an absence of political leadership and political will to build a new national consensus around the goals of social policy and citizenship equality in the 21st century. Another constraint is that Canada, already one of the most decentralized federal systems in the world, has become increasingly so. While much of the jurisdiction over the social policy terrain rests with the provinces, it is also the case that there is a need for establishing mechanisms for sharing best practices, ensuring transparency and accountability for the CST, and for promoting national goals and priorities in the social policy field.

It is recognized that the federal government is unable to either impose or enforce rigid national standards in provincial jurisdictions, yet this should not be an impediment to intergovernmental co-ordination and co-operation in the pursuit of widely held social values and policy priorities. Indeed, the federal and provincial governments agreed in the SUFA to work with other governments to develop, over time, comparable indicators to measure progress on agreed objectives, to report regularly to constituents on the performance of social programs, and to use transferred funds for their specified purpose.

These commitments provide the foundations for the development of some form of mechanism for promoting intergovernmental goal coherence in the social policy field, transparency with respect to the CST, and consultation and accountability with respect to the development, implementation and outcomes of social programs.

The open method of co-ordination was created in 2000 and is being further developed by the European Union to address these requisites for good governance within a transnational context. Recognizing that, not unlike the Canadian provinces, different European governments have different traditions, priorities and resource capacities, the open method represents a soft law (non-binding) approach to promoting both the broad social goals of the EU and transparency and accountability among its member units. The open method also involves a cyclical benchmarking procedure that co-ordinates national policies by providing guidance and assessment at the European level. The method involves a combination of collective identification of objectives, the development of national action plans, peer review of plans and procedures for addressing objectives and measuring accomplishments, joint evaluation mechanisms and best practices, and feedback for policy adjustment (Wiseman 2003).

These co-ordination procedures are referred to as open because of their potential openness to the participation of stakeholders and their openness in terms of objectives and instruments that can be adjusted more easily to changing needs than a traditional regulatory policy based on legislative standards (Smismans 2005).

Addressing the political reality of Europe and the diversity of its welfare systems, the open method of co-ordination process recognizes the political and economic difficulty of adopting social standards through regulation. Given the absence of social legislation at the European level, fundamental social rights may potentially be realized as a hard stand that open-method processes would facilitate, thereby avoiding deregulatory tendencies. With this approach, methods of co-ordination rather than regulations are used to attain policy ends. This soft law approach to governance is arguably more adaptable to variations across countries and circumstances of policy; flexibility permits respect for national diversity. Beginning in 2003, member states were required to adopt national action plans to address 18 social indicators of "social protection" (Wiseman 2003).

We suggest that the newly created open method of co-ordination may be an interesting approach to intergovernmental co-operation on social policy in the Canadian case. This approach builds on the existing SUFA. Indeed, as noted above, the SUFA already commits Canada's governments to broad social goals as well as to instrumentalities that could be adapted to create a homegrown method of interprovincial co-ordination similar to the open method. Although SUFA has been criticized for its failure, we argue that it is not the SUFA framework, per se, but the lack of political will/momentum behind it that has led to disappointing results. By adopting a type of open method of co-ordination strategy to the SUFA objectives, there may be a unique soft law approach that would contribute to greater policy coherence between budgetary decisions and the commitments to equality, poverty reduction, and human rights.

Building Links with Women through Web Development

Recommendation: Status of Women Canada should develop its web-based capacities to strengthen and develop interactive communication with individual Canadians concerned with gender issues, as well as a diverse and growing virtual women's community, and to inform and link relevant policy communities in critical debates concerning gender equality and social policy.

The worldwide web has rapidly grown into an indispensable resource for both governmental and non-governmental organizations to provide information, gain critical feedback, generate consensus, and mobilize constituencies and policy communities. Building a multifunctional virtual infrastructure would strengthen the unit's education function, foster public support and legitimacy for women's claims in the policy process, and congeal a vibrant but diffused virtual women's community.

Budgets, Capacity and Gender-Based Analysis

Recommendation: Introduce a systematic gender-based analysis of the budget process within the Department of Finance to coincide with the budget planning cycle. Three mechanisms are recommended:

- Create within the Department of Finance an external advisory group of experts on gender equality, economic policy and the use of gender budget analysis following the model of the U.K.'s Women's Budget Group and Her Majesty's Treasury.

- A gender-based analysis champion (with necessary staff supports and financial resources) within the Department of Finance would oversee an annual review of budget instructions, narratives, planning processes, indicators, benchmarks and oversight capacities within all federal line departments.

  The questionnaire in Appendix B illustrates the manner in which a dialogue within departments might be launched. This would identify the actual process of setting budget priorities, indicators and methods available, capacity to undertake analyses that includes gender and the oversight and evaluation functions that are in place. A further component of such a project would be to assess over time the budget documents and narratives of the entity in question. A series of specific exercises targeted at different actors in the budget planning process could also be developed that would show how to bring gender into the analysis and how to place social policy concerns on the same level as those related to sound macroeconomic planning.

- Enhance the capacity of gender-based units within federal and provincial governments to undertake the gender-based analysis of budgets and fiscal policy. This would include the allocation of funds to enhance the capacity of these units to scrutinize macroeconomic policies through a gender-sensitive lens.

Recommendation: In terms of enhancing the capacity of gender equality advocates outside of government, that the Department of Finance create an interactive web-based initiative that explains the budget process.

Recommendation: That the Department of Finance work with SWC to enhance its capacity to develop URL linkages with non-governmental actors committed to gender budgeting, particularly those dealing with the most vulnerable groups in Canadian society (i.e., Aboriginal women).

Recommendation: That the Department of Finance, in discussion with SWC, establish a pre-budget consultation fund for gender equality groups to give them the necessary resources to participate in the Standing Committee on Finance Hearings. Furthermore, that such groups be a part of the industry representations based on their specific areas of interest and expertise. This would prevent the separation of gender equality issues from broader industry and macroeconomic questions.

Seven

Postscript

The Harper Government and the End of Equity

WE HAVE DOCUMENTED the many ways in which the very idea of gender equity has been progressively erased from the federal government's institutional structures and policy agenda in past decades. It also offers a series of tangible recommendations that, if implemented, could help recover ground lost, as well as advance the goal of gender equity in Canada. However, it is unlikely that the present federal administration will embrace any of these recommendations. Instead, the delegitimization, dismantling, and disappearance of gender equity as a goal of public policy were dramatically accelerated with the election of Stephen Harper's minority Conservative government in January 2006 (Brodie 2008b). Shortly after taking power, the Harper government initiated a $2 billion "fat trimming" exercise. Conducted within the context of a ballooning federal surplus, the cuts were made largely at the expense of Canada's equality-seeking groups, and especially Canadian women. In the eyes of many observers, the minority Conservative government appeared bent on silencing a diverse range of governmental and non-governmental organizations that had, over the course of a generation, advocated for citizenship equality and gender equity, both in the courts and in the policy process. The Court Challenges Program (CCP), which funded individual and group challenges to public policy under the equality provisions of the Canadian Charter of Rights and Freedoms, was terminated, as was the Law Commission of Canada (LCC), which provided independent research on pressing and controversial legal questions, many of them grounded in equality claims such as same-sex marriage.

Although this fat trimming exercise also sliced through Aboriginal health, adult literacy, and youth employment programs, Status of Women Canada (SWC), the core interdepartmental agency responsible for promoting women's equality within the federal state, appeared to be the Conservative government's primary target. SWC's operating budget was cut significantly, most of its regional offices were closed, its Independent Policy Research Fund was eliminated, and funding was withdrawn from non-governmental organizations that conducted research, lobbied Canadian governments, and engaged in advocacy on behalf of women's equality. These debilitating cuts made in 2006 were followed by a further $5 million reduction to SWC's operating budget in the Harpter government's 2007–08 Estimates. Even more telling, the very word "equality" was purged from the SWC mandate and from its website.

In the fall of 2006, the Honourable Beverley Oda, then Minister of Canadian Heritage and the Status of Women, confidently informed a House of Commons standing committee that "this government does fundamentally believe that all women are equal" (quoted in Beattie 2006, A12). Oda had been called before the Standing Committee on the Status of Women to account for the Harper government's assault on Canada's gender equity agenda policy machinery. "Equality," Minister Oda explained, "is enshrined in the Charter and there was no need to repeat it in the mission statement of Status of Women Canada... Every part of the federal government has to be founded on the belief of equality," she continued, and thus the government as a whole, rather than designated agencies, was "responsible for the development of policies and programs that address the needs of both men and women" (quoted in O'Neill 2006, A17; Beattie 2006, A12). In other words, Oda advanced the "everywhere but nowhere" formula that had already been applied to the federal government's gender equity commitments.

This unilateral declaration of both women's equality and the redundancy of the federal government's gender-based policy machinery had not been telegraphed, either by Prime Minister Harper's previous commitments to Canadians to advance women's equality or by the weight of documentation, much of it emanating from the federal government itself, which pointed to the persistence of long-standing indicators of gender inequality as well as the emergence of new barriers to equality, linked to women's increased workforce participation, multiple family forms, widening income gaps, inadequate social policy supports, and ethnic and racial discrimination. During the 2006 election campaign, Harper repeatedly attempted to appease the well-founded apprehensions of the voting public about his commitment to social programs and gender equality, promising that he would "take concrete and immediate measures, as recommended by the United Nations, to ensure that Canada upholds its commitments to the women of Canada" (quoted in Young 2006, A17).

The 2006 declaration that all women are equal, by Beverly Oda, the federal minister responsible for the status of women, the removal of any references to women's equality in the mandate of swc, and the termination of funding for groups that advocate in the name of gender equality must be placed within the context of a prolonged war of attrition between the dominant neoliberal "way of seeing" and the residuals of social liberalism harboured within the "gender equality" node of the federal government. Some observers, however, predicted that this war of attrition would escalate into an outright battle with the election of a minority Conservative government in 2006. Restructured in the early 2000s, Harper's Conservative Party was built around the remnants of the old Progressive Conservative Party, the defunct Reform Party, and a diverse coalition of forces long antagonistic to social liberalism in general and gender equity in particular: among them, neoliberals, devotees of Leo Strauss, libertarians, the religious right, and advocates of "family values."

Moreover, many key members of this new regime, including Harper, had a long history of opposition to the ideas and infrastructures advanced by the post-war women's movement. Ian Brodie, for example, a political scientist with palpable libertarian leanings and appointed as Harper's Chief of Staff, was on record for denigrating the Court Challenges Program because it was "in favour of as stringent a feminist interpretation of the equality section as you could possibly have, to the exclusion of all others — they're heavily funding the one side. It happens to be the gay-rights side, the pornography side, the feminist side, the abortion side." He continued to assert that "the government here is not acting as a neutral arbiter between competing claims of what social policy ought to look like in Canada. I'm outraged as a taxpayer" (quoted in Russell 2006, 43). Similar charges had been leveled at the SWC for years by, among others, Gwen Landolt of REAL Women: "It is simply an abuse of taxpayers' money to fund only one ideology" (quoted in Greenaway 2006b, A6).

Although Harper's Conservatives were fundamentally opposed to gender equity policies, the campaign to eliminate SWC was initially spearheaded by several pro-Conservative internet blogs, including SWC's nemesis, REAL Women. Its website posted its case against SWR in the summer of 2006. "Since 1973," it stated, "the federal Status of Women has given millions of dollars to feminist-only groups on the false premise that women in Canada are victims of a patriarchal society. Although some women may be victims, the vast majority of Canadian women are perfectly capable of making their own decisions about their lives." Concerned about a potential counter-campaign in support of SWC, the website urged readers to write letters to the Prime Minister and sympathetic MPs, "in order to offset this national feminist effort to protect feminist control of Canada" (Landolt 2006). After the October reorganization, Landolt posted a celebratory missive arguing that the "cuts are only offensive to the special interest group of feminists whose views are not supported by mainstream women" (2007). Another REAL Women activist, Dianne Watts, welcomed the cuts as "a bit of fresh air" and a shift from the "narrative of victimhood." She added, "Times are changing" (quoted in Greenaway 2006a, A4).

Although the Harper government did not frame the restructuring of SWC in 2006 in such anti-feminist rhetoric, electing instead to hide its intentions behind the veil of fiscal austerity and efficiency, its actions clearly were designed to terminate the post-war gender equality agenda and to cut the transmission lines that had been cultivated between the women's movement and the federal state. As already noted, the terms "equality" and "advocacy' were erased from the terms and conditions of the SWC mandate, and replaced with an innocuous mandate of "working to promote the full participation of women in the economic, social and cultural life of Canada." The new funding guidelines explicitly prohibit the WP from providing "funding for...domestic advocacy activities and lobbying of federal, provincial and municipal governments" (SWC 2007). At the same time, the new guidelines open up the possibility for profit-seeking groups to receive WP funds, as Minister Oda explained, for such things as award events, mentorship programs, and gatherings for entrepreneurs to discuss how to improve their business.[13]

The reasons offered for these fundamental changes rehearse many of the rhetorical strategies that have been deployed against the post-war gender equality agenda and are now performed as common sense (Brodie 2008). As already noted, equality-seekers are labeled as "special interests" and their political interventions as ideology; in other words, as distorted and self-interested. A second strategy is to claim that women do not constitute a distinct political constituency with identifiable interests and needs because there is no such thing as a "women's issue." According to Canadian Heritage Minister Beverley Oda, "a lot of issues are not women's issues, they are Canadian issues...we don't need to separate men from women in this country" (quoted in O'Neill 2006, A17).

A third and related device is the assertion that there is no longer any need for separate gender-based policy machinery within the federal government. This argument is advanced on both theoretical and practical grounds. The theoretical case, one cultivated by the implementation of gender mainstreaming in 1995, asserts that SWC is redundant because, according to Minister Oda, "all ministers in our government are working for the benefit of Canadians — both men and women" (Oda 2007a, A11) and that "every part of the federal government has to be founded on the belief of equality" (quoted in O/Neill 2006, A17). The creation of SWC, Oda reasoned, actually undermined the realization of gender equality because this separate agency "relieved" other policy-makers "of responsibility for making progress on equality" (Ibid).

More than this, however, the Harper government claimed that SWC was simply an inefficient way of spending taxpayers' dollars. Speaking before the House of Commons Standing Committee Responsible for the Status of Women, Oda claimed that research and advocacy had not led to significant improvements in the lives of women: SWC was "always advocating but not effectively" (Quoted in Ditchburn 2006, A06). Thus, it was time to shift money to communities, to meaningful interventions, and to women who needed such things as mentorship and retraining (Greenaway 2006a, A4). Oda emphasized this theme in a standardized letter that was issued from her office: "The Conservative government was elected to deliver value for taxpayer dollars. Programs are being reviewed to ensure every taxpayer dollar is spent to achieve results that benefit Canadians. The savings are being invested in programs that will deliver real results in the communities where people live" (Oda 2007b, 1). The money saved from cuts to research and advocacy would be targeted to women who need help rather than to "more studies on well-know issues in inequality" (quoted in *Edmonton Journal* 2006, A6). These kinds of "meaningful" and responsible government expenditures would be targeted to women who actually need government help, particularly Aboriginal women, victims of abuse, and the elderly. For Oda, other "Canadian women know the value of a dollar. They know what good use of hard-earned money means" (quoted in *Kitchener-Waterloo Record* 2006, A3).

Minister Oda rejected any suggestion that the restructuring of SWC was designed to silence equality-seeking groups. She responded to her critics with her personal observation that, "If I know one thing about women, they will speak loudly and with great clarity" if they disagree with her government's approach (quoted in *Edmonton Journal* 2007, A7).

But, the government's cut had generated immediate criticism, especially by women speaking from social liberalism's residual. Dolly Williams, President of NAC, told its annual meeting: "The government thinks that it has found a way to silence us and our sister organizations, but...women will not stand by passively while this minority government unravels the work accomplished by the equality-seeking women's movement and its social justice allies over the past 30 years" (2006).

Similarly, Michele Asselin, president of la federation des femmes du Quebec, one of the many organizations that had its funding cut, chastised the federal government for undermining democracy. "It is fundamental to Canadian democracy," she argued, "because all groups and lobbyists aren't all equal...that's part of a democratic society to finance groups that defend rights" (CBC 2006). This reasoning was reiterated by Alia Hogben, executive director of the Canadian Council of Muslim Women. The loss of WP funding for her organization, she argued, "makes it very difficult because, if you don't lobby and you don't advocate, you're not going to make systemic changes" (Ibid). Oda's response was glib and unconvincing. "I mean the thing is that we're not stopping anyone from advocating. We are not stopping anyone from lobbying. There are many, many interest groups that still advocate, still lobby, but not on the taxpayers' dollar" (CTV 2006).

Minister Oda's defense of the restructuring of SWC is hardly the stuff of great partisan rhetoric or political vision, but these pronouncements are both critical and instructive. They represent a rupture with the gendered identities and politics of the post-war welfare state and the imposition of a genderless and individualized social imaginary as a matter of common sense. This concept dismisses both the relevance of gender difference in the calculation of public policy and the force of structures in the production and reproduction of systemic inequalities — not only for women, but for all equality seekers. This discourse attempts to relieve the neoliberal project from the challenge of mediating structural barriers, and opening spaces for systemically disadvantaged to exact strategies for redress. It is not simply space that has been diminished, but also the shared identities and idioms of equality, progress, and collective welfare, which have been advanced by the women's movement since the 1960s. In this sense, then, Canada has come to the "end of equity."

Ways of Introducing Gender Analysis Into the Budgetary Process

(The U.K. Women's Budget Group)

1. Making gender visible

Questions Explored
Who are the recipients?

Requirements
Data disaggregated by sex.

2. Auditing revenue and expenditure

Questions Explored
How are spending and revenue distributed between women and men?

Requirements
Expenditure and revenue statistics disaggregated by sex.

3. Gender impact assessment

Questions Explored

What are the implications in the long- and short-term for the gender distribution of:

- resources (money and time)?
- paid and unpaid work?

Is provision adequate to the needs of women and men?

How does policy affect gender norms and roles?

Requirements

Data on the unpaid, caring economy (i.e., a satellite account incorporating time-use data).

Micro-analytic model of income distribution, incorporating model of economic (e.g., labour supply) and other (e.g., fertility) behaviour sensitive to gender differentials.

Sensitivity to gender segregation, cultural practices and gender norms and the impact that policy has on supporting or reconstructing these.

4. Gender mainstreaming

Questions Explored

How is gender taken into account in policy formulation, design and implementation?

What priorities are given to reducing gender inequality?

Requirements

Co-operation across government agencies and across the policy process.

Awareness of the scope of gender issues and ability to search out more hidden aspects of gender inequality.

Tools to assess the aims and priorities attached to policy.

5. Benchmarking

Questions Explored

Are specific targets for gender equality being met?

Requirements

Awareness of complexity of gender inequalities when setting targets.

Ability to locate the policy and other influences on particular social phenomena.

Source: Rake (2002).

Gender Mainstreaming in the Federal Budget Process

Possible Interview Questions for Line Departments

A. Senior Management/Policy Group

1. What is your involvement in the program budget process?

2. What systems are currently in place for linking policy to program and spending priorities?

3. How does the entity ensure that financial resources directed toward targeted activities for meeting gender equality goals are adequate?

4. In what ways does senior management ensure gender factors are adequately included in the budget planning process (e.g., the budget instructions, introduction to the program budget, objective and results statements, and indicators)?

5. How does the entity ensure accountability in terms of meeting objectives in program budgets? Are current oversight systems adequate?

B. Budget/Planning Branch

Session 1: Introductory Discussions

1. Has the role of the budget/planning branch changed over the last few years, and if so, in what way?

2. To what extent is gender equality taken into account in current budget/planning processes?

3. What is an adequate level of gender mainstreaming in program budget planning and documents?

4. Has there been a move to results-oriented planning and budgeting? If so, what were the motivating factors and processes of implementation (e.g., were focal points set up in the different programs). If so, what has been the impact of this in general, and in relation to gender-equality goals in particular? For example, has an emphasis on establishing and measuring clear objectives meant that more attention has been paid to gender? Has it also meant that more attention has been paid to other crosscutting themes, such as poverty, environment and governance, and how does this compare to attention to gender?

5. How would you characterize the relations between program and budget/planning staff? In what ways do these staff liaise with each other either formally or informally? Are there regular meetings when budgets and program plans are drawn up? Is the present system of liaison satisfactory?

6. Could the gender unit/focal point be drawn in more effectively in discussions between program and budget/planning staff?

7. What oversight functions are in place or could be put in place to ensure budget documents are gender mainstreamed?

8. What do you think would be the most effective way of further main-streaming gender into the budget/planning process?

C. Gender Focal Point/Theme Group

Session 1: Introductory Discussions

1. What is the goal of gender mainstreaming for your department? Does your department have a gender equality policy and if so, how does this relate to department/program planning?

2. What definition of gender mainstreaming do you use? Is this a department-wide definition?

3. How is gender mainstreaming incorporated into the medium-term budget/planning process of your department?

4. What is your level of contact with the Department of Finance? How regular is the contact? On what issues are you consulted (e.g., drafting budgets)? Are you included in the drafting of plan or budget instructions and in reviewing submissions?

5. Is responsibility for gender analysis integrated into all divisions and operations or concentrated in a specific gender focal point (a gender unit or gender specialists)?

6. Does training promote gender mainstreaming? Are discussions of budgets part of this process?

7. In what ways can attention to gender mainstreaming support the move to results-based budgeting?

8. Is gender mainstreaming part of core budgets or extra-budgetary? Or both?

9. What do you think would be the most effective way of further main-streaming gender into the budget/planning process?

D. Program Staff

Session 1: Introductory Discussions

1. What structures are in place for facilitating program planning and decision making?

2. What is the process of writing objectives/results statements and indicators in relation to the program?

3. What provisions are in place for mainstreaming gender? How effective are these?

4. What links exist between the gender focal point and other planning units in terms of planning processes around budgets?

5. How would you characterize the relations between program and budget/program staff? In what ways do these staff members liaise with each other either formally or informally? Is the present system of liaison satisfactory?

6. How is research, both in-house and external, used in program planning?

7. What do you think would be the most effective way of further mainstreaming gender into the budget/planning process?

E. Office of Oversight/Evaluation

1. How do you evaluate whether the gender equality objectives of the department are being met?

2. What would be the most effective way to monitor and report on the extent to which gender factors were being taken into account in project/program implementation?

3. How do you monitor the extent to which gender factors are taken into account in project/ program performance?

Adapted from Beck and Bakker (2002).

Websites of Provincial Agencies

Note: All URLs *were accessed October, 2006.*

Alberta

Alberta Community Development, Human Rights and Citizenship Branch in the Department of Community Development
www.cd.gov.ab.ca/helping_albertans/human_rights/womens_issues/index.asp

British Columbia

Minister of State for Women's Equality
www.mcaws.gov.bc.ca/womens_services/index.htm

Manitoba

Manitoba Women's Advisory Council
www.mwac.mb.ca/index.html

Manitoba's Women's Directorate
www.gov.mb.ca/wd/sw.html

Council of Women of Winnipeg
www.council-wpg.mb.ca

New Brunswick

Women's Issues Branch in the Executive Council Office
www.gnb.ca/0012/Womens-Issues/index-e.asp

Advisory Council on the Status of Women
www.acswccf.nb.ca/English/acswl.asp

Northwest Territories

Government of the Northwest Territories
www.gov.nt.ca

Newfoundland and Labrador

Advisory Council on the Status of Women
www.pacsw.com/indexi.html

Women's Policy Office (Branch of the Executive Council)
www.exec.gov.nl.ca/exec/WPO/default.htm

Nova Scotia

Advisory Council on the Status of Women
www.gov.ns.ca/straw/

Nunavut

Department of Health and Social Services
www.gov.nu.ca/hsssite/hssmain.shtm

Ontario

Ontario Women's Directorate
www.citizenship.gov.on.ca/owd/index.html

Prince Edward Island

Advisory Council on the Status of Women
www.gov.pe.ca/acsw/

Interministerial Women's Secretariat
www.gov.pe.ca/tpw/iws-info/index.php3

Quebec

Secrétariat à la condition féminine
www.scf.gouv.qc.ca

Saskatchewan

Forty Years and Moving Forward...The Evolution of Women's
Programming in the Government of Saskatchewan
www.swo.gov.sk.ca/40years.pdf

Yukon

Women's Directorate
www.womensdirectorate.gov.yk.ca

Bibliography

Advisory Councils of New Brunswick, Nova Scotia, Prince Edward Island, Newfoundland/ Labrador. 1994. *Women and Social Security Reform: A Submission to the House of Commons Standing Committee on Human Resources Development.* December.

Alberta Assembly Debates. <www.assembly.ab.ca>. Accessed October, 2005.

Alesina, Alberto and Roberto Perotti. 1996. *Budget Deficits and Budget Institutions.* Working Paper Number 5556. Cambridge M.A.: National Bureau of Economic Research.

Bakker, Isabella. 1994. *The Strategic Silence: Gender and Economic Policy.* London: Zed Press/The North-South Institute.

————. 1997. *Unpaid Work and Macroeconomics: New Discussions, New Research Directions.* Ottawa: Status of Women Canada.

————. 2001. *Fiscal Policy, Accountability and Voice: The Example of Gender Responsive Budgeting.* Background Study, Human Development Report. New York: United Nations Development Programme.

————. 2005. *Gender Budget Initiatives: Why They Matter in Canada.* Alternative Federal Budget Working Paper No. 1. Ottawa: Canadian Centre for Policy Alternatives.

Bakker, Isabella and Janine Brodie. 1995. *The New Canada Health and Social Transfer (CHST): Implications for Women.* Ottawa: Status of Women Canada.

Bakker, Isabella and Stephen Gill. 2003. "Global Political Economy and Social Reproduction." In *Power, Production, and Social Reproduction.* Edited by Isabella Bakker and Stephen Gill. London: Palgrave.

Bashevkin, Sylvia. 2002. *Welfare Hot Buttons: Women, Work, and Social Policy Reform.* Toronto: University of Toronto Press.

Battle, Ken, Sherri Torjman and Michael Mendlelson. 2003. "The 2003 Budget: Political Legacy Needs Policy Architecture." Ottawa: Caledon Institute of Public Policy, February.

Beattie, A. 2006. "Feminism hits a cold shoulder." *Calgary Herald,* 5 December, A12.

Beauchesne, Eric. 2003. "Court Challenge on EI." *Edmonton Journal.* (July 28): A5.

Beauvais, Caroline and Jane Jenson. 2001. "Executive Summary." *Two Policy Paradigms: Family Responsibility and Investing in Children.* Ottawa: Canadian Policy Research Networks.

Beck, Tony and Isabella Bakker. 2002. *Assessment of Progress in Gender Mainstreaming in Programme Budgets in the United Nations System, Interim Report.* Inter-agency Taskforce on Gender Mainstreaming in Programme Budget Processes, July.

Beck, Ulrich and Elizabeth Beck-Gernsheim. 2002. *Individualization: Institutionalized Individualism and Its Social and Political Consequences.* London: Sage.

Benería, Lourdes. 1991. "Toward a Greater Integration of Gender in Economics." *World Development.* 23(1).

Boessenkool, Kenneth. 1997. *Back to Work: Learning from the Alberta Welfare Experiment.* Toronto: C.D. Howe Institute.

Brodie, Janine. 1995. *Politics on the Margins: Restructuring and the Canadian Women's Movement.* Halifax: Fernwood Publishing.

————. 2002. "The Great Undoing: State Formation, Gender Politics, and Social Policy in Canada." In *Western Welfare in Decline: Globalization and Women's Poverty.* Edited by Catherine Kingfisher. Philadelphia: University of Pennsylvania Press.

————. 2003. "Globalization, In/Security, and the Paradoxes of the Social." In *Power, Production, and Social Reproduction.* Edited by Isabella Bakker and Stephen Gill. London: Palgrave.

————. 2007. "Canada's 3'D's: Gender and Social Policy in Canada." In *Remapping Gender in the New Global Order.* Edited by Marjorie Cohen and Janine Brodie. London: Routledge.

————. 2008a. "Putting Gender Back In: Women and Social Policy Reform in Canada." In *Gendering the Nation State: Canadian and Comparative Perspectives.* Edited by Y. Abu-Laban. Vancouver: University of British Columbia Press.

————. 2008b. "We are All Equal Now: Contemporary Gender Politics in Canada." *Feminist Theory.* 9:2.

Brush, Linda. 2002. "Changing the Subject: Gender and Welfare Regime Studies." *Social Politics.* 9 (Summer).

Burt, Sandra. 1994. "The Women's Movement: Working to Transform Public Life." In *Canadian Politics.* Second edition. Edited by James Bickerton and Alain Gagnon.

Burt, Sandra and Sonya Hardman. 2001. "The Case of Disappearing Targets: The Liberals and Gender Equality." In *How Ottawa Spends, 2001–2002: Power in Transition.* Edited by Leslie Pal. Toronto: Oxford University Press.

Cagatay, Nilufer. 1998. *Engendering Macroeconomics and Macroeconomic Policies.* Social Development and Poverty Elimination Division Working Paper. New York: United Nations Development Programme.

Caledon Institute of Social Policy. 1995. *Critical Commentaries on the Social Security Review.* Ottawa. January.

————. 2003. "Accountability Versus Conditionality: the Future of the Canada Social Transfer." December.

Campeau, Georges. 2005. *From UI to EI: Waging War on the Welfare State.* Vancouver: University of British Columbia Press.

Canada. 1970. *Report of the Royal Commission on the Status of Women.* Hull: Information Canada.

————. 1994. Budget Speech. Ottawa: Department of Finance.

————. 2002. *National Child Benefit Progress Report, 2001.* <www.nationalchildben­efit.ca/ ncb/NCB-2002/toceng.html>. Accessed October, 2006.

————. nd. "About the Millennium Scholarships." <www.millenniumscholarships.ca/ en/aboutus/index.asp>. Accessed October, 2006.

Canada, CCRA (Customs and Revenue Agency). 2004. Income statistics (based on 2002 returns).

Canada, CRA (Canada Revenue Agency). 2006. "Universal Child Care Benefit (UCCB)." <www.cra-arc.gc.ca/benefits/uccb/faq-e.html>. Accessed October, 2006.

Canada, HRDC (Human Resources Development Canada). 1994. *Improving Social Security in Canada: A Discussion Paper.* Ottawa: Ministry of Supply and Services.

—————. 2002a. *Knowledge Matters: Skills and Learning for Canadians: Canada's Innovation Strategy.* Ottawa. Ministry of Supply and Services.

—————. 2002b. *Promising Practices in Employability Assistance for People with Disabilities (EAPD) Funded Programs and Services.* <www11.hrdc-drhc.gc.ca/pls/edd/ SP_AH_196_08_02.lhtml>. Accessed October, 2006.

Canada, HRSDC (Human Resources and Social Development Canada). 2006. "Employment Insurance (EI) Compassionate Care Benefits." <www.hrsdc.gc.ca/asp/gateway. asp?hr=en/ i/types/compassionate_care.shtml&hs=tyt>. Accessed October, 2006.

Canada, Standing Committee on Human Resources Development. 1995. *Security, Opportunity, and Fairness: Canadians Renewing Their Social Programs.* Ottawa: Ministry of Supply and Services.

Canada, Standing Committee on the Status of Women. 2005a. *Gender-Based Analysis: Building Blocks for Success.* Ottawa. April.

—————. 2005b. *Government Response to Gender-Based Analysis: Building Blocks for Success.* September. <http://www.parl.gc.ca/committee/ CommitteePublication.aspx? COM=8997&Lang=1&SourceId=129221>. Accessed October, 2006.

Canada, Statistics Canada. 2006. *The Daily.* March 30. <www.statcan.ca/ Daily/ English/060330/d060330a.html>. Accessed October, 2006.

Canada, SWC (Status of Women Canada). 2002. *Canadian Experience in Gender Mainstreaming 2001.* Ottawa: Status of Women Canada. <www.swc.gc-cfc.gc.ca/re-sources>. Accessed October, 2006.

—————. 2004. *Budget 2004: Status of Women Canada: Gender Equality Review.* Ottawa: Status of Women Canada. <www.swc.gc-cfc.gc.ca/resources>. Accessed October, 2006.

—————. 2005. *Gender Equity Consultation.* <www.swc-cfc.gc.ca/resources/ consultations/geso9–2005/intro e.html>. Accessed October, 2006.

—————. Status of Women Canada 2007. < www.swc-cfc.gc.ca/newroom/ news2007/0307–2_e.html>

CCPA (Canadian Centre for Policy Alternatives). nd. Web site. <www.policyalternatives. ca>. Accessed October, 2006.

CCPA 2006 (Canadian Centre for Policy Alternatives). "Women in Canada — II." Canadian Centre for Policy Alternatives Monitor, vol. 13, no. 4, 29.

CCSD (Canadian Council on Social Development). 2004. "What Kind of Canada? A Call for a National Debate on the Canada Social Transfer."

Cheung, Leslie. 2005. *Racial Status and Employment Outcomes.* Canadian Labour Congress Research Paper 34, October.

Clarke, John. 2004. *Changing Welfare, Changing States: New Directions in Welfare Policy.* London: Sage.

CLC (Canadian Labour Congress). 2003. *Falling Unemployment Insurance Protection for Canada's Unemploymented,* March.

Commonwealth Secretariat. 2002. *Gender Budgets Make Cents (Understanding Gender Responsive Budgets).* London: Commonwealth Secretariat.

Condon, Mary and Lisa Philipps. 2006. "Transnational Market Governance and Economic Citizenship: New Frontiers for Feminist Legal Theory." *Thomas Jefferson Law Review.* 28: 2.

Cryderman, Kelly. 2004. "Welfare Clients Face New Policy." *Edmonton Journal.* (March 30): A7.

Daly, Mary and C. Saraceno. 2002. "Social Exclusion and Gender Relations." In *Contested Concepts in Gender and Social Policies.* Edited by B. Hobson, J. Lewis and B. Sim. Cheltenham U.K.: Edward Elgar.

Den Tandt, Michael. 2006. "Defence Spending Gets Boost." *The Globe and Mail.* (May 3): A14.

Ditchburn, Jennifer. 2006. "Women let down, MPs tell Oda," *The Toronto Star,* 6 Oct., A06.

Dobrowolsky, Alexandra. 2004. "The Chrétien Liberal Legacy and Women: Changing Policy Priorities with Little Cause for Celebration." *Review of Constitutional Studies.* 9: 1–2.

Dobrowolsky, Alexandra and Jane Jenson. 2004. "Shifting Representations of Citizenship: Canadian Politics of 'Women and Children." *Social Politics.* 11: 2.

Dominelli, Lena. 1991. *Women Across the Continents: Feminist Comparative Social Policy.* Hertfordshire: Harvester Wheatsheaf.

Edmonton Journal. 2005. "Editorial: Families' Welfare a Proper Concern." A18.

Elson, Diane. 1995. *Male Bias in the Development Process*. Manchester: University of Manchester.

Elson, Diane and Nilufer Cagatay. 2000. "The Social Content of Macroeconomic Policies." *World Development*. 28(7).

Esping-Anderson, Gosta. 1999. *Social Foundations of Postindustrial Economies*. London: Oxford University Press.

Esping-Anderson, Gosta, with D. Gallie, A. Hemerijck and J. Myles. 2002. *Why We Need a New Welfare State*. London: Oxford University Press.

Evans, Patricia. 2002. "Downloading the Welfare State Canadian Style." In *Diminishing Welfare: A Cross National Study of Social Provision*. Edited by Gertrude Goldberg and Marguerite Rosenthal. London: Auburn House.

FAFIA (Feminist Alliance for International Action). nd. <http://www.fafia-afai.org>.

Fenwick, Tara. 2004. "What Happens to the Girls? Gender, Work, and Learning in Canada's New Economy." *Gender and Education*. 16: 2.

Fortin, Sarah, Alain Noel and France St-Hilaire. 2003. *Forging the Canadian Social Union: SUFA and Beyond*. Montréal: Institute for Research on Public Policy.

Fraser, Nancy and Linda Gordon. 1994. "A Genealogy of Dependency: Tracing a Keyword of the US Welfare State." *Signs* 19(2) (Winter).

Galloway, Gloris. 2006. "Plan Favours Stay-at-home Parents." *The Globe and Mail*. (May 3): A8.

Gazso, Amber Marie. 2005. "Gendering the Responsible Risk Taker: Social Assistance Reform and Parents' Citizenship, Market and Family Care Relations in Three Western Provinces." Unpublished Doctoral Dissertation. Department of Sociology, University of Alberta.

Geller-Schwartz, Linda. 1995. "An Array of Agencies: Feminism and State Institutions in Canada." In *Comparative State Feminism*. Edited by Dorothy Stetson and Amy Mazur. Thousand Oaks: Sage Publications.

Gray, Grattan (a.k.a. Ken Battle). 1990. "Social Policy by Stealth." *Policy Options*. 11(2) (March).

Greenaway, Norma. 2006a. "Heritage Minister under fire for dropping equality." *Calgary Herald*, 6 Oct., A4.

Greenaway, Norma. 2006b. "Women's group shuts office." *Edmonton Journal*, 22 Sept., A6.

Greenaway, Norma. 2007. "Ottawa Won't Rethink Women's Funding." 2 Feb., A7.

Harder, Lois. 2003. *State of Struggle: Feminism and Politics in Alberta.* Edmonton: University of Alberta Press.

Hatfield, Michael. 2004. "Vulnerability to Persistent Low Income." *Horizons.* 7(2).

Hoskyns, Catherine. 2005. "Mainstreaming Gender in the Macroeconomic Policies of the EU." Standing Group on the European Union Second Pan-European Conference on EU Politics, Bologna, June 24–26, 2004. <www.jhubc.it/ecpr-bologna/docs/179.pdf>. Accessed October, 2006.

Hunsley, Terrance. 2006. "Work-Life Balance in an Aging Population." *Horizons.* 8(3): 3–13.

Jennissen, Therese. 1996. "The Federal Social Security Review; A Gender Sensitive Critique." In *Remaking Canadian Social Policy: Social Security in the Late 1990s.* Edited by Jane Pulkingham and Gorden Ternowetsky. Halifax: Fernwood.

Jenson, Jane. 2003. "Redesigning the Welfare Mix for Families: Policy Challenges." Ottawa: Canadian Policy Research Networks Discussion Paper. February.

—————. 2004. "Catching Up to Reality: Building the Case for a New Social Model." Ottawa: Canadian Policy Research Networks.

Kershaw, Paul. 2004. "Choice Discourse in BC Child Care: Distancing Policy from Research." *Canadian Journal of Political Science.* 37(4).

Kitchen, Brigitte. 2005. "Life-Chance Guarantees: A New Agenda for Social Policy." Toronto: Centre for Social Justice.

Kitchener-Waterloo Record. 2006. "Women's groups funding slashed; in drastic change, Tories will no longer support advocacy, lobbying." 5 October, A3.

Klein, Seth and Andrea Long. 2003. *A Bad Time to Be Poor: An Analysis of British Columbia's New Welfare Policies.* Vancouver: Canadian Centre for Policy Alternatives.

Kunz, Jean and Jeff Frank. 2004. "Poverty: Thy Name is Hydra." *Horizons.* 7(2).

Laghi, Brian. 2005. "East Coast Premiers Lobby for a New Deal on Daycare Dollars." *The Globe and Mail.* (October 29): A3.

Lahey, Kathleen. 2005. *Women and Employment: Removing Fiscal Barriers to Women's Labour Force Participation.* Ottawa: Status of Women Canada, November.

Landolt, Gwen. 2006. "Counter Attack by Feminists." [Online] Available at: www.realwomenca.com/alerts.htm#aug07_06

—————. 2007. "Hearings by Status of Women Committee a Hoax." [Online] Available at: www.realwomenca.com/press.htm#02_08_07

LCC (Law Commission of Canada). 204. "Is Work Working: Work Laws that Do a Better Job." Discussion paper. December.

Lister, Ruth. 2004. *Poverty*. Cambridge U.K.: Polity Press.

Macdonald, Martha. 1995. "Feminist Economics: From Theory to Research." *Canadian Journal of Economics*. 28(1).

Mackenzie, Hugh. 2006. The Art of the Impossible: Fiscal Federalism and Fiscal Balance in Canada. Canadian Centre for Policy Alternatives, July. <www.policyalternatives.ca>. Accessed October, 2006.

Makarenko, Jay. 2005. *The Canadian Federal Budget*. <www.mapleleafweb.com/ features/ economy/budget/Federal-Budget/>. Accessed October, 2006.

Malloy, Jonathan. 2003. *Between Colliding Worlds: The Ambiguous Existence of Government Agencies for Aboriginal and Women's Policy*. Toronto: University of Toronto Press.

Matas, Robert. 2005. "B.C. Revamping Welfare-to-Work," *The Globe and Mail.* (August 17): A6.

McIntosh, Tom. 2004. "Intergovernmental Relations, Social Policy and Federal Transfers after Romanow." *Canadian Public Administration*. 47(1) (Spring).

McKeen, Wendy. 2003. *Money in Their Own Name: The Feminist Voice in the Poverty Debate in Canada.* Toronto: University of Toronto Press.

MacLeod, L. 2006. "Tories not muzzling women: Oda." *Ottawa Citizen*, 7 Oct., B5.

Meagher, Sharon and Patrice Diquinzio (eds). 2005. *Women and Children First: Feminism, Rhetoric, and Public Policy*. Albany: State University of New York Press.

NCW (National Council of Welfare). 2002. *Welfare Incomes 2000–2001*. (Spring).

—————. 1995–2004. *Welfare Incomes*. Ottawa: Minister of Public Works and Government Services. <www.ncwcnbes.net/htmdocument/principales/online/pub-e. htm>. Accessed November, 2006.

Neysmith, Sheila and M. Reitsma-Street. 2005. "Provisioning: Conceptualizing the Work of Women for 21st Century Social Policy." *Women's Studies International Forum*. 28.

Noel, Alain. 2002. "A Law Against Poverty: Quebec's New Approach to Combating Poverty and Social Exclusion." Ottawa: Canadian Policy Research Networks Background Paper. December.

─────. 2003. "Power and Purpose in Intergovernmental Relations." In 2003. *Forging the Canadian Social Union: SUFA and Beyond*. Edited by Sarah Fortin, Alain Noel and France St-Hilaire. Montréal: Institute for Research on Public Policy.

Noel, Alain, France St-Hilaire and Sarah Fortin. 2003. "Learning from the SUFA Experience." *Forging the Canadian Social Union: SUFA and Beyond*. Edited by Sarah Fortin, Alain Noel and France St-Hilaire. Montréal: Institute for Research on Public Policy.

Norton, Andrew and Diane Elson. 2002. *What's Behind the Budget? Politics, Rights and Accountability in the Budget Process*. London: Overseas Development Institute, June.

Oda, Beverley. 2007a. "Aiming to Improve Women's Lives" *Ottawa Citizen*, 2 Feb., A11.

Oda, Beverley. 2007b. correspondence from B. Oda, 5 Feb.

O'Neill, J. 2006. "Status of Women equality mandate did the opposite, minister says." *Montreal Gazette*, 13 December, A17.

PSAC, Public Service Alliance of Canada 2006, 'Cuts to SWC,' [Online] Available at: www.psac.com/issues/womenequality/20061206c-e.shtml

PACSW, Newfoundland and Labrador Advisory Council on the Status of Women, 2004. <http://www.pacsw.com/indexi.htm>

Parkinson, Rhonda. 2002. *The Bank of Canada*. <www.mapleleafweb.com/features/ economy/bank-canada/index.html>.

Paterson, Stephanie, Karine Levasseur and Tatyana Teplova. 2004. "I Spy with My Little Eye ...Canada's National Child Benefit." In *How Ottawa Spends: Mandate Change in the Paul Martin Era*. Edited by Bruce Doern. Montréal: McGill-Queen's University Press.

Philipps, Lisa. 1996. "The Rise of Balanced Budget Laws in Canada: Fiscal (Ir)Responsibility." *Osgoode Hall Law Journal*. 34(4) (Winter).

─────. 1999. "Taxing the Market Citizen: Fiscal Policy and Inequality in an Age of Privatization." *Law and Contemporary Problems*. (Autumn). <www.law.duke.edu/ journals/lcp/articles/lcp63dautumn2006>. Accessed November, 2006.

─────. 2006. *Gender Responsive Tax Policy Making: What Would It Look Like in Canada?* Paper prepared for the Levy Institute, Bard College, April 26.

Phillips, Susan. 2003. "SUFA and Citizen Engagement: Fake or Genuine Masterpiece." In 2003. *Forging the Canadian Social Union: SUFA and Beyond*. Edited by Sarah Fortin, Alain Noel and France St-Hilaire. Montréal: Institute for Research on Public Policy.

Prince, Michael. 1999. "From Health and Welfare to Stealth and Farewell: Federal Social Policy, 1980–2000. In *How Ottawa Spends: Shape Shifting: Canadian Governance Toward the 21st Century*. Edited by Leslie Pal. Toronto: Oxford.

—————. 2002. "The Return of Directed Incrementalism: Innovating Social Policy the Canadian Way." In *How Ottawa Spends: The Security Aftermath and National Priorities*. Edited by Bruce Doern. Toronto: Oxford.

—————. 2003. "SUFA: Sea Change or Mere Ripple for Canadian Social Policy." In *Forging the Canadian Social Union: SUFA and Beyond*. Edited by Sarah Fortin, Alain Noel and France St-Hilaire. Montréal: Institute for Research on Public Policy.

Rake, Katherine. 2002. "Gender Budgets: The Experience of the UK's Women's Budget Group." Paper prepared for the conference, Gender Balance Equal Finance. Basel, Switzerland, March.

Rankin, Pauline and Jill Vickers. 2001. *Women's Movements and State Feminism: Integrating Diversity into Public Policy*. Ottawa: Status of Women Canada.

Rice, James. 1995. "Redesigning Welfare: The Abandonment of a National Commitment." In *How Ottawa Spends, 1995–96: Mid-life Crises*. Edited by Susan Phillips. Ottawa: Carleton University Press.

—————. 2002. "Being Poor in the Best of Times." In *How Ottawa Spends: The Security Aftermath and National Priorities*. Edited by Bruce Doern. Toronto: Oxford.

Rice, James and Michael Prince. 2004. "Martin's Moment: The Social Policy Agenda of the New Prime Minister." In *How Ottawa Spends: Mandate Change in the Paul Martin Era*. Edited by Bruce Doern. Montréal: McGill-Queen's University Press.

Roy, F. 2004. "Social Assistance by Province, 1993–2003." *Canadian Economic Observer*, 11–010: 3.1–3.7.

Russell, F. 2006. "Harper's cuts are designed to keep neocons on the top." *Canadian Centre for Policy Alternatives Monitor*, vol. 13, no. 6.

Sawer, Marian, 2006. "From Women's Interests to Special Interests: Reframing Equality Claims." In *The Politics of Women's Interest*. Edited by Louise Chappell and Lisa Hill. Abingdon, U.K.: Routledge.

Sen, Gita. 2000. "Gender Mainstreaming in Finance Ministries." *World Development.* 28(6).

Smismans, Stijn. 2005. *How to Be Fundamental with Soft Procedure? The Open Method of Coordination and Fundamental Social Rights.* Research Unit on European Governance Working Paper 2/2005. Turin, Italy. <www.urge.it>. Accessed October, 2006.

Statistics Canada 2006, *Women in Canada: A gender-based statistical report.* Ottawa: Statistics Canada.

Summers, Anne. 2003. *The End of Equality: Work, Babies and Women's Choices in the 21st Century.* Sydney: Random House.

Stetson, Dorothy and Amy Mazur (eds). *Comparative State Feminism.* Thousand Oaks: Sage Publications.

Stratigaki, M. 2004. "The Cooptation of Gender Concepts in EU Policies: The Case of 'Reconciliation of Work and Family.'" *Social Politics.* 11(1).

Teghtsoonian, Katherine. 2005. "Disparate Fates in Challenging Times: Women's Policy Agencies and Neoliberalism in Aotearoa/New Zealand and British Columbia." *Canadian Journal of Political Science.* 39(2).

Teghtsoonian, Kathy. 2004. "Neoliberalism and Gender Analysis Mainstreaming in Aotearoa/New Zealand." *Australian Journal of Political Science.* 39(2).

Teghtsoonian, Kathy and Joan Grace. 2001. "Something More is Necessary: The Mixed Achievements of Women's Policy Agencies in Canada." In *State Feminism, Women's Movements and Job Training.* Edited by Amy Mazur. New York: Routledge.

Torjman, Sherri. 1995. "Milestone or Millstone? The Legacy of the Social Security Review." Ottawa: The Caledon Institute of Social Policy.

Townson, Monica. 2005. *Poverty Issues for Canadian Women.* Prepared for Gender Equality Consultations. Ottawa: Status of Women Canada. August.

United Kingdom, Her Majesty's Treasury. 2004. *Gender Analysis of Expenditure Project: Final Report.* <www.womenandequalityunit.gov.uk/research/gender_analysis.pdf>. Accessed October, 2006.

Voyer, J.P. 2004. "Poverty and Exclusion: New Perspectives, New Approaches." *Horizons.* 7(2).

Weldon, Laurel. 2004. "Citizens, Victims, Deviants: Restructuring Government Response to Violence Against Women in Canada." Paper presented at the Annual Meeting of the American Political Science Association, Chicago.

Williams, Dolly. 2006. "NAC condemns changes to Status of Women Canada Mandate." [Online] Available at: www.newswire.ca/en/releases/archive/October2006/13/c8089. html?view=print

Wiseman, Michael. 2003. "The European Union's 'Open Method of Coordination' and Social Policy in the United States: Are There Connections? Opportunities?" Paper prepared for seminar by Sr. Frank Vandenbroucke, Belgian Secretary of State for Employment and Pensions, George Washington University, Elliot School of International Affairs, October 27.

Yalnizyan, Armine, 2005a. *Canada's Commitment to Equality: A Gender Analysis of the Last Ten Federal Budgets (1995–2005)*. Ottawa: Canadian Feminist Alliance for International Action.

—————. 2005b. "Assessing the Federal Budget 2005: What's in It for Women." Paper prepared for the Feminist Alliance for International Action. Ottawa. March.

—————. 2005c. "Divided and Distracted: Regionalism as Obstacle to Reducing Poverty and Inequality." Ottawa: Canadian Centre for Policy Alternatives, September.

Young, M. 2006. "Women let down: Government cuts to Status of Women Canada budget betray our UN commitments and Harper's words." *Vancouver Sun*, 7 Dec., A17.

Notes

1. As quoted in Brodie (1995: 58).

2. As quoted in Jennissen (1996: 240).

3. As quoted in Teghtsoonian and Grace (2001: 250).

4. As quoted in Jennissen (1996: 240).

5. As quoted in Galloway (2006: A8).

6. Hansard February 7, as quoted in Yalnizyan (2005c: 19).

7. The Ontario government announced it is discontinuing this practice, beginning by not clawing back the July 2004 increase to the NCBS.

8. New Brunswick, it should be noted, introduced a demonstration project called New Brunswick Works in 1993. Aimed at increasing employability and self-sufficiency, participation in the program was voluntary. In 2000, it introduced a new program that provides wage subsidies to employers that provide 26 weeks of employment to designated individuals.

9. As quoted in Noel (2002: 5).

10. As quoted in SWC (2002: 1).

11. As quoted in Lister (2004: 79).

12. Balanced budget laws and indeed, constitutional amendments, introduce a specific set of numerical targets into the budget process, limiting for instance, the standard Keynesian anti-cyclical policy prescription of tax cuts, expenditure increases and deficits in recessions with tax increases and expenditure cuts and surplus during expansionary periods. Several critical points have been raised concerning the relationship between balanced budget laws and the alleviation of poverty (Philipps 1996; Bakker 2001). First, balanced budget laws reflect a questioning of the feasibility of fiscal fine tuning. These statutes and laws are meant to institutionalize an era of limited government by constraining governments in their fiscal policy decisions (i.e., range of policy choices as Philipps documents, 1996: 689) by establishing caps in spending and taxation. In doing so, however, they discourage proactive policies to promote equality of incomes since balanced-budget legislation, in particular, is likely to generate increased pressure for regressive spending cuts whenever revenues decline. In times of recession, the political costs of spending money to eradicate poverty or to address the human impacts of restructuring may be perceived as prohibitively high by politicians. Second, balanced-budget laws undermine the crucial role that government spending plays in stabilizing the economy during private sector recessions. Without the ability to engage in counter-cyclical spending, governments will have to meet a fall in levels of demand through spending cuts, a strategy which might well postpone recovery (Philipps 1996). In sum, it can be argued that this aspect of balanced budget laws reveals an important political dimension (i.e., a bias in favour of limited government and against redistributive fiscal transfers) (see also Norton and Elson 2002).

13. In the Spring of 2007, the WP was further restructured to include a Women's Community Fund, which provides meager resources for community groups to provided services to targeted groups of women, such as aboriginal women, victims of abuse, and senior women, and a new Women's Partnership Fund, which provides seed money for groups to leverage resources through community partnerships.

The production of the title **Where are the women?** on Rolland Enviro 100 Print paper instead of virgin fibres paper reduces your ecological footprint by :

Tree(s) : 1
Solid waste : 36 kg
Water : 3 384 L
Suspended particles in the water : 0,2 kg
Air emissions : 79 kg
Natural gas : 5 m³